BEHIND
THE
SCENES

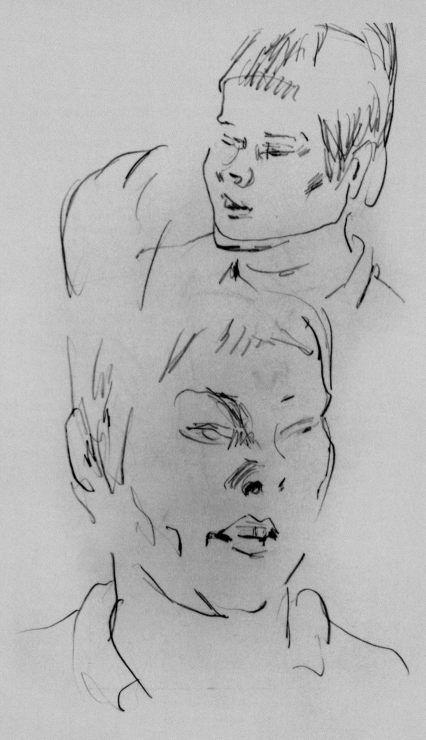

Sketch by Cecil Beaton, 1969

BEHIND
THE
SCENES

JUDI DENCH

With an Introduction by John Miller

St. Martin's Press
New York

Preface

So much seems to have happened to me in the last ten years. I have been to India twice, to film *The Best Exotic Marigold Hotel* and its sequel, both directed by John Madden. I have played 'M' three more times, and was not best pleased when they killed me off in *Skyfall.*

I made my first film in Hollywood, directed by Clint Eastwood, who was charming, and in many ways unlike any other film director I have known. I met one of my great heroines Sophia Loren for the first time when we worked together on the film *Nine,* and joined a host of old friends in *The Cranford Chronicles* for TV.

I loved revisiting Ireland when we filmed *Philomena* because my mother was born in Dublin and my father grew up there. Steve Coogan was fun to work with, and we had lots of laughs between takes. I met the real Philomena, whose story we were telling, which was a great help in capturing her strong character.

In the theatre I also enjoyed playing a richly varied group of strong women – Judith Bliss in *Hay Fever,* Mistress Quickly in *The Merry Wives of Windsor,* Titania again (half a century after I first played her), and Alice Liddell in *Peter and Alice.*

I await the next offers on stage or screen with interest. My eldest brother, Peter, is always trying to persuade me of the joys of retirement, but that plays no part in any of my future plans. Since my husband Michael died in 2001 I have worked constantly. Friends and colleagues are very sustaining; they are the people who get you through it – it's no good to be on your own.

Looking again at these pictures brings back many happy memories; yet they also remind me of quite a number of gaps in my experience which I would like to fill. All my life I have tried hard to avoid being typecast or pigeonholed, and whenever anyone says, 'Oh, you shouldn't play that part,' it only makes me much more determined to try.

I want to do something different next, and preferably something dangerous. Of course I have enjoyed playing some parts more than others, and which are which will become apparent in the pages that follow. Some made me laugh more than others too, and surprisingly often these were in tragedies.

I would like to thank Alan Samson at Weidenfeld & Nicolson for inviting me to put together this second photo album, ten years after I put together the first *Scenes From My Life*, and John Miller for once again helping me by recording my memories of some of the most rewarding experiences of my life, as well as of so many people who have been important to me in different ways.

Introduction

I first saw Judi Dench onstage in 1961 as a touchingly vulnerable Anya in the RSC production of *The Cherry Orchard*; the first time I worked with her was in 1994, when I interviewed her for my BBC Radio Ninetieth Birthday tribute to John Gielgud. He had played Gaev opposite her in that Chekhov play, and she was forever grateful to him for restoring her self-confidence when the director Michel Saint-Denis had nearly destroyed it by treating her dismissively. Our shared admiration of the great actor paved the way for my biography of Judi in 1998 and other work together since, some of which is pictured in this book.

She was the first to agree to appear in the Gielgud Centenary Gala at the theatre named after him, which I produced for the American Shakespeare Guild in 2004; her acceptance was swiftly followed by those from an all-star cast. When I asked her which Shakespeare scene she wished to play she said immediately: 'Oh, *The Dream* with Ian Richardson as Oberon again, I could go on as Titania now, I've never forgotten those lines.' That was still true in 2010: when she reprised the part for Peter Hall at the Kingston Rose Theatre he didn't bother to call her for the first week's rehearsal, while the rest of the

cast learnt to be as word-perfect as her. I saw her as Titania in each of those productions half a century apart, and was enchanted by her performance on both occasions, as I have been so often in the years between.

It was seeing her as Lika in Frank Hauser's production of *The Promise* with Ian McKellen and Ian McShane in 1966 that made me realise here was a truly great actress, destined to become the acknowledged leader of her profession, in direct line of succession to Ellen Terry, Sybil Thorndike, Edith Evans and Peggy Ashcroft.

Since the publication of my biography in 1998 I have been privileged to share a stage with her on several occasions to discuss her career, at the National Theatre, the Royal Shakespeare Theatre at Stratford, and various literary festivals, all of which sold out well beforehand. This confirmed Peter Sallis's remark to me: 'Judi Dench is the number one box office draw in this country, male or female.'

The most challenging request she made was to create a comic recital for her on the theme of Great Eccentrics, which we performed as a three-hander twice at the Winchester Festival, once with Michael Pennington, and once with Charles Dance. As we came offstage on the second occasion she handed me her script, saying: 'That's the last recital I'm ever going to do, I can't now read the script properly, even blown up in size as you've done.'

That was the first inkling I had of her macular degeneration of the retina, a development which we managed to keep to ourselves for quite a while, until one Saturday morning when the *Daily Mirror* splashed the story right across its front page. Judi was furious, as the 'exclusive' leak was then picked up by the rest of the media, here and abroad. I had several concerned calls from friends in America asking if it was true. Ironically, she was filming a Bond movie at the time, but 'M' never caught the culprit. We worked out that someone on the film crew must have overheard her discussing her sight problem with a friend in the cast, and sold the story to the paper.

She hasn't let this change get her down, and even cited the advantages when she appeared at the Royal Albert Hall in the Promenade Concert devoted to the work of Stephen Sondheim. She sang 'Send in the Clowns' from *A Little Night Music,* and said how glad she was that she couldn't see the faces of the audience, 'They just looked like a sea of waving cornflowers in the distance.'

Neither has the problem stopped her from working. She has changed her method of learning a part, by listening to it on tape instead of reading it off the page. In the theatre that means she has to know her lines on the first day of rehearsal, which Ben Whishaw, her young co-star in *Peter and Alice,* told me was a touch embarrassing for the rest of the cast still holding their scripts in their hands. But it meant they all worked hard to learn their parts much quicker than usual. Ben was only the latest of a long line of Judi's leading men to have told me how stimulating and rewarding it was to play opposite her – from Ian Richardson and Robert Hardy in the early 1960s to Billy Connolly and Jim Broadbent more recently.

It is hard to credit now that Judi was told after her first screen test: 'Miss Dench, you have every single thing wrong with your face.' She has spared that purblind producer's blushes over the years since by always refusing to name him, but it rather put her off screen-acting until recent years. Her Oscar nomination for *Mrs Brown* opened the floodgates, and leading film-makers now queue up to seek her services. Typically, when Clint Eastwood rang her up at home to ask her to play J. Edgar Hoover's mother in his next film, she assumed it was her friend Brendan O'Hea pulling her leg.

I mentioned John Gielgud at the beginning, and I remember asking him why he vetoed the ninetieth birthday tributes planned by the theatre world and by his club The Garrick. He said then: 'Oh, if they make too much fuss about me being ninety, they'll all think I've retired, and stop offering me work.' His fears were of course groundless, and he filmed his last performance just a month before his death, aged 96.

Judi has always expressed her similar determination never to retire, so I look forward to collaborating with her on another book of reminiscences in another decade or so. Until then, I hope you will enjoy turning the pages of this one as much as I have enjoyed helping my dear friend Judi to put it together.

John Miller

Every night at the Old Vic I watched each play in the season from the wings. I learnt so much from watching others.

First Fairy in *A Midsummer Night's Dream*, Old Vic, 1957

The love of acting is in the family blood. My father was a keen amateur actor, both my brothers acted at school and I followed my brother Jeffery into drama school. I suppose it was only natural that my daughter Finty should want to follow her parents into the profession. Though she initially wanted to be an acrobatic nurse!

My first ambition was to be a dancer. I was always dancing everywhere. I can remember very clearly my father saying when I can't have been very old, 'The thing about being a dancer is that before you get to forty probably you won't be able to go on dancing, you'll have to do something like teaching it.' Even then, that was my idea of hell, and that really put me off. I don't like the thought of anything packing up. Until then I was really quite serious about wanting to be a ballet dancer.

In this picture I am not conforming to anybody, I'm afraid, and if you look very closely you can see that I have extremely scabby knees where I was always falling down. When I was a child, going to bed early in the summer was agony for me. I have such a vivid memory of hearing the boys playing cricket outside in the garden, then running up and down the stairs because somebody'd forgotten something and had to fetch it. Then friends would come over and you would hear a lot of laughing, then it would go quiet for a minute and you knew they had all gone off to somebody else's garden. I couldn't bear to miss it. I don't want to be part of the action necessarily, but I don't want to miss anything. I don't mind if I'm just sitting on the side, so long as I'm hearing it. I don't want to miss a lot of larks.

On my right is my friend Ursula Gayler, who was later my dresser at the National Theatre.

This is me on holiday in France with my brother Jeffery, my father and my sister-in-law Daphne.

This is the earliest picture I have of my husband Michael (right) –
you can already see his mischievous sense of humour.

Michael (top row, centre) with five of his school friends and then with
four of the same group on his fiftieth birthday. They all remained close
friends throughout their lives.

The *York Mystery Plays* were revived in 1951 and were performed every three years, directed by E. Martin Browne. Daddy played Annas the High Priest. He was a very good actor as well as a very good doctor and my ma was in charge of making all the costumes, designed by Norah Lambourne. We had auditions at school, and I got in, playing an angel.

There were about eight of us from the Mount, and we were allowed out of school to take part. That was a terribly exciting time. Tenniel Evans played the Archangel Michael. He then went to Colchester and he wrote to me all the time he was there; we had a wonderful long correspondence until I was about eighteen. Next time I played the angel sitting at the door of the tomb in white clothing. Henzie Raeburn, E. Martin Browne's wife, refused to let me have anything to sit on, so I had to crouch for a long time.

Here we are during a rehearsal break in 1951. I am third angel from the right, listening to Tenniel Evans.

York Mystery Plays, 1951

At this time I thought I wanted to be a designer, and between my second and third appearance in the *York Mystery Plays* I went to art school. Then I was taken to see Michael Redgrave's *King Lear* at Stratford, so brilliantly designed by Robert Colquhoun, with a huge saucer and a rock, which became, in turn, the throne, the cave and everything else. I'd never seen anything like it and I felt I was very old-fashioned about what I had previously thought. It was a Road to Damascus moment for me. But still, when I come to do a play, the bit I like best is when they show me the set and the costumes.

Finally, I ended up playing the Virgin Mary in the *Mystery Plays* in 1957.

The Virgin Mary, *York Mystery Plays*, 1957

My parents gave me a twenty-first birthday party which was held at Queen Alexandra's House, by the Albert Hall, near where I was living when I was a student at the Central School of Speech and Drama, and the actor Jeremy Kemp was also a student at the same time. On another night, when Jeremy and I were late back from seeing dear family friends John and Jean Moffat, the door was locked and we sat on the doorstep the entire night, until the door was opened in the morning. Jeremy stayed with me – gallant to the last.

The best work, in my experience, is always done where there is a genuine company spirit. That was something I learnt to treasure with my very first company at the Old Vic, and have since usually managed to achieve in my seasons at Nottingham and Oxford, and subsequently with the RSC and the National Theatre. This photo shows some of us who were in the Old Vic Company at the end of the 1950s. I am on the left, then Maggie Smith, Moyra Fraser, Alec McCowen, Rosemary Ackland and John Moffatt.

I adore this picture of Daddy in my dressing room at the Old Vic after a performance of *Hamlet*. He came to most of my performances. When I played Juliet I had a line 'Where are my Father and Mother, Nurse?' and he was the one who shouted out: 'Here we are darling, in Row H.'

For *Hamlet* I had this absolutely beautiful costume, designed by Audrey Cruddas: green shot with silver, and greyish silver beads. She set it in the Ruritanian period and all the chaps wore what we used to call shoes for tall girls – slip-on pumps. I got very bad notices for Ophelia. It did me a lot of good. If you get bad notices the first thing you do, it doesn't half bring you up with a jolt. When the Vic toured America it was decided that Barbara Jefford should play the part. That was hard to bear, but I was lucky enough to be playing Maria in *Twelfth Night* and the Princess of France in *Henry V*.

John Neville was playing Hamlet, and there is nobody who can hold a candle to John for leading a company – nobody I've ever met. He was brilliant at teaching you basic things that I don't think young actors are taught anymore – the whole business of getting in on time, being prepared, and not taking up the director's time while you sort out the problem of what is actually your homework. He had a great sense of fun, which is terribly important, and there's no doubt that if a company is led like that it comes over to an audience that it is a unit which works together. It's something you can't manufacture.

John used to hate it if anyone said they were tired and he's quite right. Acting requires discipline, and if they are too tired well, frankly, I feel they should let someone else do it. When I caught Asian flu during *Hamlet* at the Old Vic, one night I cried during the scene and went to pieces, and John came off and said, 'If you can't do it, let your understudy. Don't go on and show something that's nothing to do with Ophelia.'

I thought that was a very good lesson to learn.

Ophelia in *Hamlet* with John Neville, Old Vic, 1957

I had a blonde ponytail as Phebe in *As You Like It* – what an arse-paralysing part! When the audience is shifting about and finding their handbags, ready to go home, suddenly she comes on again, having a row with Silvius. 'Oh good grief,' they all think, 'not another two having a row!' I'm bottom left, with John Stride as Silvius.

One night during *The Importance of Being Earnest* Fay Compton, as Lady Bracknell, said, 'Thirty-four is a very attractive name, Mr Cardew.' Alec and I laughed so much we were told off by Fay; we were really given a rocket. When I told John Gielgud much later, he said, 'How dare she. She was absolutely frightful at laughing on the stage.'

TOP Phebe in *As You Like It*, Old Vic, 1959

OPPOSITE Cecily in *The Importance of Being Earnest* with Alec McCowen as Algy, Old Vic, 1959

Romeo and Juliet was a great success. It was Franco Zeffirelli's first Shakespearean production and he was quite unlike any other director I ever worked for.

John Stride and I were in our twenties though, as you can see in the opposite photo, we looked much younger. We had a marvellous time doing it.

TOP Franco Zeffirelli adjusts my costume

BELOW With Barbara Leigh-Hunt during the technical run. Her wig had obviously been taken away to be dressed during one of the waits.

OPPOSITE Juliet in *Romeo and Juliet* with John Stride as Romeo, directed by Franco Zeffirelli, Old Vic, 1960

One day in rehearsal for *Twelfth Night* Michael Benthall said to me, 'Could you play it in a dialect?' and I said, 'Yes, I'll play it Yorkshire' and it fitted actually very well. Joss Ackland played Sir Toby on the American tour and he introduced me to jazz. Several of us went to hear Kid Ory, Earl Hines, Louis Armstrong and Billie Holliday.

Maria in *Twelfth Night* with Joss Ackland as Sir Toby Belch, Old Vic, 1958

Isabella in *Measure for Measure* with Tom Fleming as the Duke, Stratford, 1962

With John Gielgud and Dorothy Tutin in *The Cherry Orchard*, Aldwych Theatre, 1961. John said that Dottie and I were like the two daughters he might have had. What a lovely man as well as a great actor.

When we were rehearsing *Measure for Measure* at Stratford I used to cycle out to Tom Fleming's cottage at Hampton Lucy for breakfast. I would collect the cream and Tom would have the porridge on, then we'd put the bike in the car and come in to rehearsal. On Shakespeare's birthday we were invited to that big civic lunch, and the beadle said, 'Name?' and Tom said, 'Tom Fleming.' The man announced 'Mr Albert Finney' and then he said to Tom, 'A horse, a horse, my kingdom for a horse.' We never did find out what that was all about.

At the same time as being at Stratford I was commuting to the Aldwych. I was doing *The Dream* and *Measure for Measure* at Stratford, and the TV of *Major Barbara* in London. We seemed to be going up and down the road from London to Stratford about three times every other day. We thought nothing of it, and there was no M40 then.

I met Raymond Mander and Joe Mitchenson when I was at the Old Vic, and they used to take me to the Players' Theatre and lots of First Nights. They were hugely good fun and they took me everywhere. Their house was full of theatrical treasures, and they let me hold the Order of the Elephant that William Macready wore round his neck as Hamlet in the nineteenth century, which you can see in that wonderful portrait of him. They were so sweet, and they knew absolutely everybody. I was with them the night I first met my future husband Michael: he was in *Celebration* at the Duchess Theatre and he came to join us in the pub afterwards in Covent Garden. It was also through them that I met the Edwardian actress Ada Reeve, who was a friend of Ray's and Joe's.

ABOVE With Raymond Mander and Joe Mitchenson

OPPOSITE With Ada Reeve

One of the happiest times I had was at Oxford and making a friend of Frank Hauser. I did several seasons at the Playhouse for him, with great friends like James Cairncross. He was a brilliant director and I once said, 'If Frank asked me to step in front of a bus, I'd do it.'

Irina in *Three Sisters* with James Cairncross as Solyony,
Oxford Playhouse, 1964

Denholm Elliott presenting me with a BAFTA Award for Most Promising Newcomer in *Four in the Morning*. That was a great surprise, as I wasn't very lucky in my early film career. I've still got that dress.

Four in the Morning was shot in Deodar Road in Putney, directly under the flight path, directly next to the road bridge, directly next to the railway bridge, and opposite where they dumped the rubbish on the river. We never got a take for longer than a minute and a half. It was just after the shooting of this film that my father died. Norman Rodway came round for a cup of tea, and it was while he was there that my brother Peter rang to say Daddy had died. It was 1 December 1964.

Jude in *Four in the Morning,* 1965

What thou seest, when thou dost wake,
Do it for thy true-love take.

I had one happy reconciliation during the run of *The Dream.*
Franco Zeffirelli had been furious with me for refusing to join
the Old Vic American tour of *Romeo and Juliet,* because I went
to join the RSC in Stratford instead. But now I had a letter
from him, saying, 'Seeing how clever you've been in Stratford
I have completely forgiven you for having abandoned Juliet.
You know I've missed you deeply, I've hated you immensely
– now I see that altogether you were right.'

So that was good news.

Titania in *A Midsummer Night's Dream* with Ian Richardson as Oberon
and Ian Holm as Puck, Stratford, 1962

We had rather different costumes for the film of *A Midsummer Night's Dream*, or rather hardly any at all. The leaves for our costumes were picked in the morning, and we wore green welly-boots, as I was frightened of worms.

When Peter Hall suggested I play Titania again forty-five years later I said to him: 'Peter, I can't do that again,' and he said, 'Of course you can.' He set up an opening scene of the company all arriving at Court, with me as Queen Elizabeth. They designed the most wonderful ass's head for Bottom, quite adorable.

It was lovely working with Peter again. He is such a stickler for getting the rhythm of Shakespeare's verse right, which is always such a great help. My grandson Sammy came to the First Night, and sat absolutely motionless throughout, as he has at every Shakespeare play from when he was very young.

OPPOSITE Titania in *A Midsummer Night's Dream*, Kingston Rose Theatre, 2010

ABOVE With Peter Hall in rehearsal

Noël Coward came to see *Private Lives*, but thank goodness he wasn't there on the First Night. My bracelet flew off into the audience, the lid came off the coffee-pot and Teddy put it in his top pocket; he pushed me into the top of the trolley, I couldn't get out and he wouldn't help me. It was the most riotous First Night I've ever experienced.

John Neville directed *Measure for Measure* and gave it a very different setting from the one at the RSC. It was in modern dress and the moated grange was now a nightclub. When I asked John, 'How do I come into this nightclub?' he just yelled at me, 'The way any nun comes into a nightclub after hours.'

ABOVE Amanda in *Private Lives* with Edward Woodward as Elyot, Nottingham, 1965

OPPOSITE Isabella in *Measure for Measure* with Edward Woodward as Lucio, Nottingham, 1965

Rehearsing a dance routine for a charity fundraiser with other actresses at the London Palladium in July 1963. From left to right: Peggy Lummins, Sylvia Syms, Janette Scott, Anna Massey, Liz Fraser, Eunice Gayson, Hayley Mills, Juliet Mills, and me.

St Joan, Nottingham, 1966

When we were delayed in Act II at the Dress Rehearsal of *St Joan* I was standing in the Green Room, and I looked out of the window and saw a woman with two children and a whole lot of bags pushing a pram. I turned and looked at all this knitted chain mail on everyone and I thought, 'Oh God, what are we doing?'

> *It is at the hour, when the great bell goes after 'God-will-save-France': it is then that St Margaret and St Catherine and sometimes even the blessed Michael will say things that I cannot tell beforehand.*

Lika in *The Promise* with Ian McKellen and Ian McShane,
Oxford Playhouse, 1966

The Promise was a wonderful play, by Alexei Arbuzov, but it's nearly three hours long with only three actors and lots of costume changes. I used to drop off to sleep when Frank Hauser was giving us notes. There was a big bed I used to curl up on and Frank would say, 'Is she awake? Because I have a few notes.'

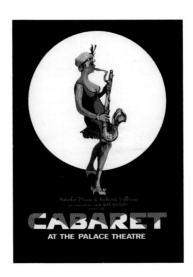

Hal Prince saw me in *The Promise* and my agent Julian Belfrage rang to say that Hal Prince wanted to see me for his production of *Cabaret*. I said, 'You have to be joking.' So Julian took me out to lunch, I bought a feather boa, drank two glasses of wine, and when I arrived at the theatre I sang from the wings. I was so frightened. Amazingly I was cast as Sally Bowles! I went for singing lessons to Gwen Catley and after she'd heard me she said, 'Well, yes, you're not a singer.'

I said, 'Well, I know.'

'But I can teach you to sing in your way.'

It was Hal who said to me, 'Read the book *Goodbye to Berlin*, and read what it says about her.' Of course, the thing about Sally Bowles is that she isn't a singer, she's a middle-class girl from England who's gone out to Berlin. She can't sing. She could never be a success.

Sally Bowles in *Cabaret*, Palace Theatre, 1968

The musical director was going to New York while we were rehearsing and he said, 'Is there anything you want me to bring back?'

'Yes, the top note from the end of *Cabaret*.'

Hal overheard me and he said, 'If you can't get the top note, act that you can't get it.' That suddenly released me. The one thing that Sally Bowles craves to be is a star, but it's the one thing she's not, she's a failure.

I loved doing it, I loved working with Hal. When I was starting rehearsals I was sitting in my agent's garden in Primrose Hill with that beautiful actor David Hutcheson and he asked, 'Have you had the band call yet?'

'No.'

'When you have it, the hair on the back of your neck will stand up.'

He was so right, and it's not only at the first band call, but for ever afterwards.

During the overture, when you are standing at the back waiting to go on, it's just so exciting.

I loathe taking curtain calls. It embarrasses the hell out of me. I begged Hal Prince not to have one in *Cabaret*, because I thought it would be so wonderful to have that train going away and everyone going with it.

OPPOSITE Celebrating with Lila Kedrova after our First Night performance of *Cabaret*, 1968. Champagne is my only drink.

Trevor Nunn asked me to play Hermione in *The Winter's Tale* and I was very shocked. I said, 'Good God, Trevor, all those juveniles have gone by, and it's mothers' parts already?'

'Yes, I'm afraid it is.'

Then about three weeks later he said, 'Actually, how would you like to play her daughter Perdita as well?' That had last been done in Forbes Robertson's production with Mary Anderson. The extraordinary coincidence is that the day before Michael and I married a few years later, the critic John Trewin sent us a wedding present and inside was a picture of Mary Anderson playing Hermione. He told us, 'What you might be interested to know is that while she was doubling Hermione and Perdita, the only person to do that before you, she got married. Not only did she get married in London, but she got married in the same little church in Hampstead that you are getting married in tomorrow.' Michael told the story in his speech.

I love that kind of continuity, of something being passed down, I love being able to pass something on. What upsets me about now is that I think the majority of young actors don't really want to know our great theatre tradition. I just think how lucky to be given the chance of playing great parts that other actors before you have played. So hopefully one is carrying on a great tradition, and I'm very aware of that. I feel that so strongly because of working with Peggy Ashcroft, John Gielgud and Edith Evans. They were all in a line with earlier actors.

TOP Perdita in *The Winter's Tale* with David Bailey as Florizel, Stratford, 1969

BOTTOM Hermione with Richard Pasco as Polixenes

During the run of *Twelfth Night* Roger Rees and I invented a game called 'Ferret in the foot', also known as 'Badger in the boot' or 'Rabbit in the ruff', which had to be indicated with the appropriate action by different members of the cast. I don't think anyone in the audience noticed, but it was very exciting, and it didn't half get you through that interminable last scene.

Donald Sinden invented a wonderful piece of business on his entrance in cross-garters: he walked forward and looked at the sundial, then he looked at the sun, then he checked his watch, then he moved the sundial.

Viola in *Twelfth Night* with Donald Sinden as Malvolio, Stratford, 1969

Michael flew out to Australia when we were touring with *Twelfth Night* for the RSC and proposed to me in Adelaide. I said, 'No, it's far too romantic, with all this sun and the beaches. Ask me again one rainy night in Battersea.' So he did, and I said 'Yes' this time, and we got married in the middle of winter – on 5 February 1971.

Tina Carr was a photography student when she took all these pictures of our wedding, when my brother Peter gave me away.

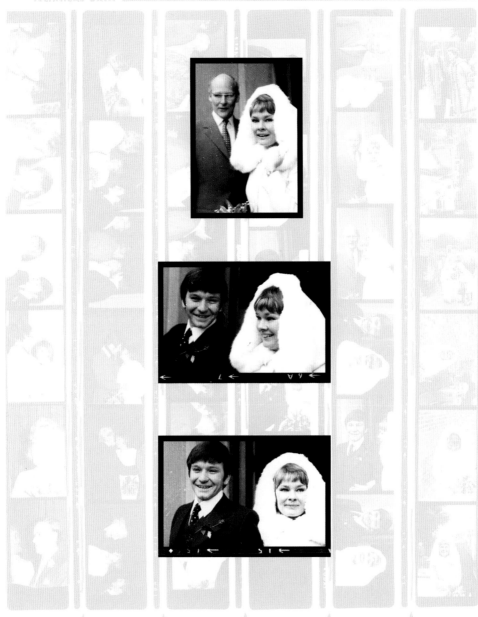

Michael seemed to think my going-away hat suited him as much as me, and I love this picture of him in it.

Trevor Nunn gave me and Michael a lovely advance wedding present by casting us as young lovers in *London Assurance*. Here I am in my dressing room during the run. I had a lovely friend in Nottingham called Brian Smedley, who's a judge, and he'd asked me to marry him. I'd said, 'May I let you know?' The next time I saw him I was about five months pregnant. He just put his head round the door and said, 'I take it the answer's no?'

I met the actress Cathleen Nesbitt not long after I was married, at a cocktail party at the Savoy Hotel. She was so beautiful, and you can see why Rupert Brooke wrote all those letters to her.

Portia has a speech to Bassanio in the Caskets Scene in *The Merchant of Venice*:

> *I speak too long, but 'tis to peise the time,*
> *To eke it out, and to draw it out in length,*
> *To stay you from election.*

One night I said, 'To stay you from erection', absolutely boldly and out front. Well, the wind band left the stage. My brother Jeffery, Bernard Lloyd and Peter Geddes all left. And I laughed. Michael had a great long speech as Bassanio. I've never seen him use his hands so much and turn his back to the audience; it was terrible.

I had this idea of a wig with lots of curls, and John Neville came to see it. I hadn't seen him for years, and he knocked on the door and said, 'Hello Bubbles.'

That's all he said to me, and quite right too.

Portia in *The Merchant of Venice* with Michael Williams as Bassanio, Stratford, 1971

After our daughter Finty was born I was prepared to give up work altogether, but Michael preferred that I didn't. Fortunately I managed to get work in the theatre when she was tiny, so I was going to the theatre when she was going to bed, then later I did television during the day while she was at school, and had the evenings off, so I didn't miss out on anything.

We were in Cyprus to shoot a magazine promotion for the
TV series *Love in a Cold Climate*. There was a wonderful pool
at the Dome in Kyrenia and the sea just washed into it. This
natural sea pool, with crabs rushing across the bottom, was
the most conducive place for learning to swim – warm and
clear and sandy on the bottom. Finty learnt to swim in just
two days. She is as keen on swimming as I am and is wonderfully good at it.

Our extended family at Charlecote, near Stratford-upon-Avon,
taken when Finty was three

It was so perfect. Michael's parents and my ma, Michael, Finty
and me – all living together in one house. My mother and
Michael's parents all got on well together, so, a couple of years
after Finty was born, Mike said, 'Wouldn't it be wonderful if
we could all just live together?' That was absolutely my idea
of heaven; it's like a Quaker community, both for bringing up
a child and the whole idea of looking after your parents. It
appals me more than anything else in this country how the
elderly are shot off somewhere where they sit like zombies in
a room, and they're there to die.

This is a terrible picture of my ma. Michael's father is
standing next to her. The very lifelike doll we gave Finty
was called Daisy. Once, at an airport, Finty was walking
along dragging Daisy by the arm and some Austrian woman
came up saying, 'It's terrible what is happening to that baby,
dragging it along the floor, it is shameful!'

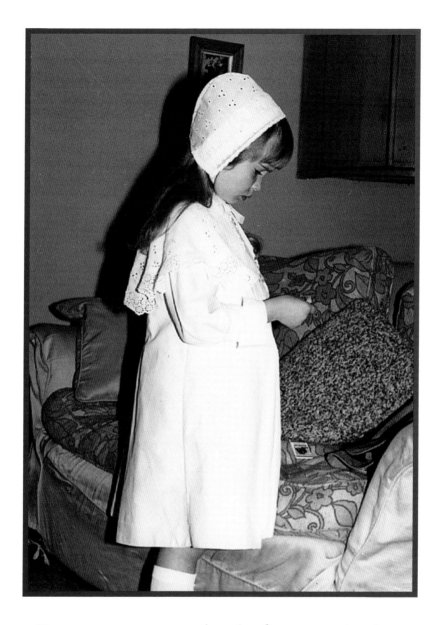

Finty was very, very cross about her first communion dress, because all the other children were got up as brides in long white dresses and veils. I found this lovely Victorian dress and I made the bonnet, and Finty never quite forgave me for the costume. I thought she looked just terrific in it.

I have to be able to laugh in rehearsal. I don't want to work with anybody who hasn't got a sense of humour, it's too boring, and that goes for directors too. It's too tedious. There are certain aspects you have to take seriously, but the moment you start taking yourself seriously, and you can't laugh at yourself or see the funny side of something, I think pack your bag.

During rehearsals for *Too True to be Good* we all went to lunch at Joe Melia's house in Primrose Hill, and his wife Flora had a terrible headache, so I said, 'We all ought to go out and find a rare thing on Primrose Hill, and bring it back.' Ian McKellen and Joe brought back a park bench.

I adored playing alongside Donald Sinden in both *London Assurance* and *Much Ado*. He is such a funny man. I had an argument with Peggy Ashcroft about Beatrice, because I think there is tremendous melancholy in her, and she didn't see any melancholy at all. Because Donald and I weren't in our twenties or thirties, we made it a last-chance summer that they could possibly get together. There is something very leftover about Beatrice. As she says, 'He played me false once.' She actually alludes to that, so I took that as my guide, that she was hurt badly and didn't want to go there again.

TOP *Too True To Be Good* with Joe Melia, Aldwych, 1975

CENTRE AND BOTTOM Beatrice in *Much Ado About Nothing* with Donald Sinden as Benedick, Stratford, 1976, and in rehearsal with Donald Sinden and John Barton

I've never believed that one should suspect Lady Macbeth from her first appearance in *Macbeth*. I don't agree with Edith Evans that there must be a scene missing, I can't see what it would say that isn't already in the play. I said to Trevor Nunn one day, 'We must do it so that any schoolchildren who come to see it and don't know it will think that that they may not do the murder.' We all take so many things for granted.

We did it at The Other Place at Stratford, which was then just an old building with a corrugated iron roof that used to creak and groan. Trevor got the stage management to put little pieces of paper in every single chink of light there was, and as an exercise he sent Ian McKellen up some stairs and said, 'Judi, wait at the bottom, and Ian come down the stairs, knowing there are people asleep all around you.' That completely unblocked something for us.

Trevor decided to do it without an interval, and we sat round in a circle on old orange-boxes, a very minimalist set, and all our costumes were very plain. On the First Night there was an unbelievable storm throughout the sleepwalking scene, which sent gusts of wind under the door so the candle flickered, so it was effects by God, really.

We had no understudies at The Other Place, so when Roger Rees broke his ankle he had to play Malcolm in a wheelchair. At the opening of the play Susie Dury, who played one of the Witches, used to dribble slightly and drag her foot, and two of the court used to raise Duncan up and help this aged person forward. So, after Roger had come on in his wheelchair, Marie Kean, the First Witch, passed me and whispered, 'It's the Lourdes production!'

We were weeping with hysteria, I don't know how we got through it.

Lady Macbeth with Ian McKellen as Macbeth, The Other Place, Stratford, 1976

The middle girl is wondering how she can play the rest of this part! I should never have taken the role of Regan in *King Lear*. I blame Mike Gwilym and Nick Grace for putting me off the part. I had a long fur coat, very Zhivagoesque, in which I thought I looked very chic, until they said, 'If you run in that fur coat somebody will take a pot-shot at you.'

Regan in *King Lear* with Marilyn Taylerson as Cordelia
and Barbara Leigh-Hunt as Goneril, Stratford, 1976

Here I am in rehearsal with John Woodvine and Barbara Leigh-Hunt. We have our *Lear* faces on. That rehearsal room is now the Swan Theatre.

> CORNWALL *Seek out the traitor Gloster.*
>
> REGAN *Hang him instantly.*
>
> GONERIL *Pluck out his eyes.*

I found it very hard to take the physical cruelty in Regan.

We were never so fit as during this production of Trevor Nunn's musical based on *The Comedy of Errors*, because of the class exercises that the brilliant choreographer Gillian Lynne put us through every morning. The open-air taverna in John Napier's set looked like something out of a travel brochure for Greece, and I have never had so many letters from schoolchildren.

It was enormously good fun. At the end we invited the audience up on the stage to dance along with us. When we took it to Newcastle the audience wouldn't go home. We finally had to say, 'Would you mind going home, we have to get back to our hotel?' Those children's letters showed how this production transformed their view of Shakespeare, and converted them to want to come again.

On the last night John Woodvine as Dr Pinch entered from the audience, saying 'You stay there, Aphrodite.' When I said 'Good Doctor...' he replied 'I'm not a Good Doctor, I don't have the patients.' That was funnier on the stage than it is on the page.

Adriana in *The Comedy of Errors*, Stratford, 1976

BOTTOM left to right: Richard Griffiths, Nickolas Grace, Roger Rees, Francesca Annis, me, Mike Gwilym, Michael Williams

Cymbeline was a difficult play, and this was my most difficult moment, when I woke up beside Bob Peck's headless body. The dummy's knees weren't made accurately, and kept bending the wrong way.

Imogen in *Cymbeline* with Ben Kingsley as Iachimo, Stratford, 1979

THE SUNDAY TIMES, JANUARY 22 1978

THE ARTS

Sally Soames

Judi Dench and Michael Pennington rehearse the roles of Millamant and Mirabell for Tuesday's opening of Congreve's "The Way of the World" at the Aldwych. The RSC's new production is directed by John Barton and designed by Maria Bjornsen. Beryl Reid joins the company to play Lady Wishfort, with John Woodvine as Fainall

The restoration comedy *The Way of the World* was the first time I played opposite Michael Pennington. Here we are struggling in vain to work out the plot, and I don't think any of us understood it. But we had great fun with it. John Woodvine had to hand someone something to sign and one night, instead of handing him a quill pen, he handed him a whole bird.

When we were rehearsing Sean O'Casey's play *Juno and the Paycock* I was finding it very difficult at one point and I said to Trevor Nunn, 'Haven't you got some mangy old cat that I could play in this musical you're going to do?' I said it as a joke and then I was cast as Grizabella; I was also going to play Gumby Cat, but I never played either of them in the end, because I snapped my Achilles tendon.

In costume for *Cats*, 1980

OPPOSITE Juno in *Juno and the Paycock*, with Gerard Murphy as Johnny Boyle, Aldwych, 1980

We had many holidays camping in the west of Scotland. One year we got so soaked that all our changes of clothes were soaked too. Then I remembered that Tom Fleming had recently performed the opening ceremony of a hotel for Robin and Sheena Buchanan-Smith on the Isle of Eriska. He said, 'It's a wonderful place, you'll all love it.' So we went and threw ourselves on their mercy and they said, 'Of course we'll dry everything off and you can stay.'

The next day they said, 'Go off and have a lovely day; we've got another place for you to pitch your tent.' In fact we were put up in their house in Lymphoy and that's how that friendship began, and our love of Eriska. We've been going there ever since. We used to pile up the lilos and duvets in the back of the car, and Finty used to clamber in and just sleep on top of them all while we listened to the children's stories on the radio. She slept her way all round Scotland. We both have such vivid memories of being in our sleeping bags in our tent, and Michael sitting with a lamp and a vodka, reading us ghost stories. We had great times in the tent, until Finty suddenly developed a wish for a warmer beach. We were in a loch way up on the west coast of Scotland and it was paralysingly cold. Michael was shouting at us from the shore, 'You don't have to do this, you know, you are on holiday.'

With Peter Hall in rehearsal for *The Importance of Being Earnest*

JUDI   Are you sure she can be played at this age?

PETER   I don't want you to say that again.

I had no idea how to play Lady Bracknell. Peter Hall gave me two weeks off during rehearsals and we took the car up to Scotland and stopped at Inveraray for lunch on the way up. I looked at the Castle and thought of Margaret, Duchess of Argyll, with that very pale face, dark hair and red mouth. It was a great clue. There's also a quality in Lady Bracknell that could be quite predatory. She is so awful about Lord Bracknell and was always dying to get round to Half Moon Street to put her hand on Algy's knee. I had a more coquettish hat made, with a whole bird in it.

One night I skipped the line 'A handbag?' and I saw the whites of Martin Jarvis's eyes! But he exquisitely came to the rescue and I don't think many of the audience noticed the omission, even though it's crucial for the last scene and the play. I got one indignant letter from a lady who said I'd ruined Christmas for her.

Lady Bracknell in *The Importance of Being Earnest* with, top, Nigel Havers as Algy and, above, Martin Jarvis as Jack Worthing, Lyttelton Theatre, 1982

Here I am on location in Thailand filming *Saigon: Year of the Cat* with my co-star Freddie Forrest outside the US Embassy, and with the director Stephen Frears. Freddie had worked with Marlon Brando, who taught him to improvise his own lines instead of speaking those in the script. This didn't go down very well either with David Hare or Stephen Frears.

We had a scene where we were evacuated in a helicopter, and the day before we shot it a helicopter had crashed on that very airfield, so Stephen hid the newspapers from me. I would, in fact, have taken comfort from that, because if it's going to happen one day, it's unlikely to happen the next, is it?

The photo below was taken at Charlecote when I had just got back from filming. Finty came out to Thailand for a while to stay with me and we had a lovely time; it was where she learnt to dive.

I have always loved living in the country. We were thinking of moving from Charlecote when our parents were no longer with us, and Michael saw a picture of this house in *Country Life*. He sent off for the details without telling me, but as soon as we walked inside we knew it was just what we wanted. It's an old farm-house with oak beams, which are a bit of a hazard to my taller friends, and we have been so happy here. Even when I am playing nightly in the theatre in London I like to come back here every night.

We bought Henry, our first Shih-Tzu for Finty when she was little. We had to call him Henry, because we saw him in a shop in Sloane Street. He was adorable, and used to come and sit in at rehearsals (sometimes!) with me. Now we have another Shih-Tzu called Minnie.

I was making a TV film about York, where I was born. I took Finty to my school, and the Shambles, and the Minster. The film was called *Judi Dench looks at York* or some such title. I have never actually seen it.

OPPOSITE: Returning to York with Finty

Laura in *A Fine Romance* with Richard Warwick, Susan Penhaligon and Michael, 1980

My first situation comedy, *A Fine Romance*, was directed by the divine Jimmy Cellan-Jones, who wore sandals the whole time, even in the snow. We were rehearsing in the church by Waterloo Bridge, and it was our wedding anniversary in February. Michael went to the flower seller under Waterloo Bridge and said, 'Could I have some roses?'

'Roses!!? D'you know what time of the year it is, mate!?'

When I was singing one day in that church, the verger came up and said, 'Don't do that.' I never forgot that. Stop singing in church!

I adored playing Barbara in *Pack of Lies*, but it was very difficult. She was a very quiet and restrained person, so I found it difficult to pitch the performance to the back of the circle. Michael broke your heart.

Barbara in *Pack of Lies* with Michael Williams as Bob, Lyric Theatre, 1983

Mother Courage and Her Children with Zoe Wanamaker, Bruce Alexander
and Stephen Moore, Barbican, 1984

I had clearly in my mind that the wig should be red and look as if just anybody had cut it, so it was always standing on end. When I said this to the costume designer Lindy Hemming on the first day, she produced the design she had already done with red hair exactly like it. But the rehearsals didn't really work for me until I found Michael's old coat that he had worn in *Schweyk in the Second World War*.

Amy O'Connell in *Waste* with Daniel Massey as Henry Trebell, Barbican, 1985. I lost my voice at the opening, until Cicely Berry brought it back with some special vocal exercises, to everyone's great relief, especially mine.

The design for the BBC's production of *Ghosts* was very stark. The only colour on the set was a great big pile of green apples. This was the first time I worked with Kenneth Branagh, who played my son Oswald. Ibsen's play is a sombre one, as Mrs Alving discovers that her son has inherited syphilis, but we had one moment when we laughed so much we were sent home in disgrace. Elijah Moshinsky wanted to put the opening titles over a panning shot round the dining table with a music track. We were asked to improvise a conversation that would only be heard under the music as a murmur. Natasha Richardson as the maid came round with a dish of potatoes, and offered them first to Michael Gambon, who said: 'I'll just have the usual twelve.' Ken and I couldn't contain ourselves and corpsed helplessly. Elijah's voice came over the tannoy: 'Thank you Mr Branagh, Miss Dench, you can leave the studio, thank you, we've got that.'

Mrs Alving in *Ghosts* with Michael Gambon as Pastor Manders, Natasha Richardson and Kenneth Branagh, directed by Elijah Moshinsky, 1985

Mr and Mrs Edgehill was filmed for the BBC in Sri Lanka and I said I could go, but Finty's birthday came in the middle of it and I was reluctant to be away at this time. Alan Shallcross offered to fly me home, as long as I worked right up to the moment I got on the plane, and worked the moment I came back. We had a wonderful birthday party and I brought Finty back some sapphire earrings. When I got back I was on the set within minutes of arriving. They built a beautiful house for us on the shore, which, of course, was demolished later. It was the most wonderful setting.

Mr and Mrs Edgehill with Ian Holm, 1985

Mr and Mrs Edgehill, 1985

I did *The Browning Version* with Ian Holm in 1985 for television.
I love this picture because it doesn't look like me;
it just looks like the character.

Michael as Dr Watson to Clive Merrison's Sherlock Holmes,
BBC Radio, 1989

This was a publicity shoot for *Radio Times* and the only time Michael and Clive ever had to dress the part. It was a great partnership and the two of them were so brilliant together; the series ran for ages. They recorded a comic parody in which Sherlock Holmes confesses his secret love for Watson, which was never broadcast, but was played at Michael's memorial service.

OPPOSITE Michael in *September Song*,1993. I love this picture of Michael, and he had a huge success in that part.

Ned Sherrin was lovely to work with on *Mr & Mrs Nobody*: precise, and funny, and very, very astute, then suddenly he'd sit back and say, 'Look out, the Williamses are on automatic pilot.'

We thought it was going to be a doddle, a really short evening, get a lot of laughs and straight home, but it was desperately hard work. However, working in those very heavy costumes meant I lost a lot of weight before I tackled Cleopatra.

Carrie Pooter in *Mr & Mrs Nobody* with Michael as Charles Pooter, Garrick Theatre, 1986

It is interesting but often quite hard returning to plays from your youth in the more mature parts, moving from Ophelia to Gertrude, and Anya to Madame Ranevskaya – both had such echoes for me – and I couldn't get Peggy Ashcroft's performance in *The Cherry Orchard* out of my mind. But Cleopatra was such a challenge. I said to Peter Hall, 'I do hope you know what you're doing, casting her as a menopausal dwarf.'

I will never forget what Peter said to me about playing Cleopatra, I have passed it on to so many people. He said, 'Don't ever think you have got to play all aspects of the character in every scene. Just choose one thing. At the end of the evening it might add up to the full person. The other thing' – which would never have even occurred to me – 'is don't imagine that when other characters speak about you, they are telling the truth.'

He gave the example of Enobarbus (which was so wonderfully played by Michael Bryant at the National) getting back to Rome, and that scene is really about him in the bar with his mates. 'Come on, tell us, what's she like?' He is telling a tale.

Cleopatra in *Antony and Cleopatra*, Olivier Theatre, 1987

Cleopatra in *Antony and Cleopatra* with Anthony Hopkins as Antony,
Olivier Theatre, 1987

OPPOSITE Red Nose Day for *Cleopatra*. No, I did not wear it on stage!

At Buckingham Palace with Finty and Michael the day I received my DBE, 1988.

Johnny Mills was an incorrigible practical joker, worse than me. When we were in the musical of *The Good Companions* together, there was an actor in the company who was not behaving very well, so Johnny suggested that we put stage weights in his suitcase for the Going Away number. He couldn't lift the suitcase, let alone swing it about. John and I were both told we were amateurs.

The night he and Mary invited Michael and me to join him for supper at Overton's after the show he caught me by surprise when he handed me the menu onstage to place my order in advance, as the kitchens would be closed when we got there. I told those stories at his memorial service in June 2005, which was a very nostalgic occasion, as we all remembered what a lovely man he was.

This photograph of him, Michael and me was taken at his eightieth birthday celebration.

That's me on the right in the photo above. We have always done lots of aqua-ballets, from the Nottingham West African tour in the mid-1960s, at the big pool in Kaduna when we completely emptied it of people, to another on a rough day in the sea at Dubrovnik, while we were on tour with *Hamlet* with the National Theatre.

The Cherry Orchard has such memories for me of Peggy Ashcroft when we were at the Aldwych. Playing Anya first, then following Peggy as Ranevskaya, and all those echoes of John Gielgud and everybody. It was impossible to clear my mind of how Peggy had played it.

Michael Gough gave a radio interview just after we opened and said, 'I am working with three of the most attractive women in the West End.' So when he arrived at the theatre that evening I got together Miranda Foster, Lesley Manville, Abigail McKern and Kate Duchene, and we all lined up in front of him. I said, 'OK, Michael, who are the three?' We never let him forget that!

ABOVE Ranevskaya in *The Cherry Orchard* with Miranda Foster as Anya, Aldwych, 1989

OPPOSITE With Michael Gough as Firs

Hamlet with Daniel-Day Lewis, Olivier Theatre, 1989. I thought, I'll try and play Gertrude like Jill Balcon, Dan's mother, very tall and dark, but I never succeeded!

We couldn't get through the first reading of *The Sea*, we laughed so much. With twenty minutes of the play to run after our final exits Celia Imrie and I used to drink a small glass of champagne in the wings before the curtain call. Mrs Rafi was a deeply unpleasant character, and I got a letter from somebody saying how dare I call the play a comedy. They had come after a funeral and had expected to see something rather different. Mrs Rafi was a monster, but it was hugely good fun to play her.

Mrs Rafi in *The Sea* with Karl Johnson and Christabel Dilks, Lyttelton Theatre, 1991

Ken Branagh asked me to direct him as Jimmy Porter in *Look Back in Anger*. It was put on for just one week in Belfast, to raise funds for charities in Northern Ireland. We only had two weeks' rehearsal, which was very short.

Look Back in Anger, 1989. Left to right: Edward Jewesbury, Emma Thompson, me, Kenneth Branagh and Gerard Horan

I look as if I'm about to produce a rabbit from under my shawl. We had a nice time at Chichester performing *Coriolanus*, except for the night I fell over onstage and couldn't get up. They had to stop the play and ask if there was a doctor in the house. Fortunately there was, and he strapped up my sprained ankle, so I finished the performance leaning on a stick. At the curtain call Ken usually came on last, but this night he leapt out first, and then with an exaggerated gesture led me out to a great wave of sympathetic applause. I was rather overwhelmed by the ovation, until Ken restored my equilibrium by hissing 'Get off the stage, you limping bitch!'

ABOVE left to right: me, Kenneth Branagh, Susannah Harker

OPPOSITE Volumnia in *Coriolanus* with Kenneth Branagh, Chichester, 1992

The Gift of the Gorgon was one of the most difficult plays I ever had to tackle. It had wonderful reviews, and Finty was so bowled over by it that she couldn't come round afterwards. Because of the names of our characters, and the fact that Michael and I had played Mirabell and Millamant, we always refer to ourselves as Mr and Mrs Plum.

Mr & Mrs Damson with Michael Pennington in *The Gift of the Gorgon*, Barbican and Wyndham's Theatre, 1992

Ken Branagh admired Sir John Gielgud as much as the rest of us, and proposed this Renaissance co-production of *King Lear* to BBC Radio 3 to mark Sir John's ninetieth birthday on 14 April 1994. He assembled a wonderful all-star cast, including Simon Callow, Derek Jacobi, Norman Rodway, Iain Glen, Sheila Hancock, Ian Holm, Richard Briers, Nicholas Farrell, Maurice Denham, Barbara Leigh-Hunt and Samantha Bond. Even Peter Hall was persuaded to play the tiny part of the Herald. Ken played Edmund, and I was Goneril.

With Anthony Page in rehearsal for the TV production of *Absolute Hell*, 1991

I so enjoyed doing *Absolute Hell* for television that I said to Tony Page, 'Wouldn't it be lovely to do this in the theatre?' Four years later he and I did it at the National, with a different cast.

My favourite play, *Absolute Hell*, had been savaged by the critics at its premiere in 1952 and neglected since. The author Rodney Ackland came along to see the TV recording just before he died, and he said to me very touchingly afterwards, 'I didn't realise I had written such a good play.'

This picture says it all about the character. I would like to be going to do that play tonight. In the nightclub we were only drinking coloured water, but Greg Hicks and I used to get completely stotious, rolling about on the floor. It was like one endless party.

I loved Peter Woodthorpe so much, ever since we were together at the RSC. He was wonderful as Toad. When he played the Doge in *The Merchant of Venice* he said to us, 'Well, I'm having a strop, because Terry Hands has put me in this chair, and they can't see the cut of my costume.' He sat in it all through lunch, as a protest!

OPPOSITE Christine Foskett in *Absolute Hell*, and with Peter Woodthorpe in rehearsal, Lyttelton Theatre, 1995

I fell down twice during the run of *A Little Night Music*. In 'You Must Meet My Wife' there was one moment where Larry Guittard was crossing towards the band and I slipped, he turned round to face me and he couldn't find me. I was underneath the chaise longue.

A Little Night Music, Olivier Theatre, 1995

You start to play a part and you get so immersed in it, trying to get it right, that you forget the responsibility of being passed that part to play, because it takes up all your energies and all your anxieties. We had a very merry time doing it.

Brendon O'Hea and I developed 'Sixteen Going on Seventeen' as our cabaret act for the party after the last night of *A Little Night Music* at the National, and then we did it at this club near Seven Dials for the charity West End Cares. We had a very good time, but we mustn't do it anymore, because I am now sixteen going on eighty, as Brendan keeps reminding me.

'Miss Dench you have every single thing wrong with your face.' That was the crushing verdict of the film producer who gave me my very first screen test back in the 1950s. It put me off films for a long time, and my few early excursions into the cinema did little to change my mind. Television seemed to be much more fun, from an early *Z-Cars* episode to the later situation comedies I so enjoyed. Even my first big-screen success – *Mrs Brown* – began life as a project for TV.

This was the most difficult scene in *Mrs Brown*. It took twenty-one takes because the horses misbehaved, and my heavy skirts kept getting caught on the pommel as Billy Connolly lifted me down, and then our radio mics became entangled. It was a very important scene too, as it's their closest moment in the entire film, when the Queen refuses to let John Brown resign:

I cannot allow it because I cannot live without you.
Without you, I cannot find the strength to be who I must be.

If Billy was nervous there was no sign of it. He was just fantastic from the word go. At the end of a day's filming we'd all go off for showers, then we'd meet in the bar and have a drink, and Billy would sit down with a pot of tea on a tray in front of him, and then sometimes he'd just start telling stories. I would be looking at my watch and thinking, 'Can I do tomorrow's filming on just five and a half hours' sleep?' We'd be absolutely weeping with laughter, and I'd look at my watch again and think, 'Can I do it on four and a half hours?'

Queen Victoria in *Mrs Brown* with Billy Connolly as John Brown, 1997

ABOVE John Madden, the director, watches us rehearse

Half the local gentry turned out to play the staff at Balmoral in *Mrs Brown*, as the extras had to be able to dance the Eightsome Reels expertly. Billy Connolly danced it as if to the manner born.

Rather fittingly, Finty played Princess Helena, one of
Queen Victoria's daughters.

Sammy hated his kilt when he was dressed for the part at Billy's.
'Off skirt, off,' he kept saying, as soon as we put it on him. It was
a bit better when he got the skean dhu. Now he's fine about it.

With Michael and Finty at the premiere of *Tomorrow Never Dies*, 1997

I never thought about what a huge responsibility I had in playing 'M'. I think I was just really excited about it, and Michael and Finty were absolutely mad about it – 'a Bond-woman.' It was lovely working with Pierce Brosnan. I didn't get to any exotic locations, not in seven Bond films. All I got was Stowe School, very nice but not abroad, and a trailer labelled Innsbruck.

M in *The World is Not Enough* with Pierce Brosnan as Bond, 1999

Situation comedy is the most difficult thing I've ever done. You don't get a preview, you get one chance to get it right. In *A Fine Romance* Michael had a sure touch about it, he used to know exactly, and Geoffrey – if you want to know about playing comedy on television, just look as far as Geoffrey Palmer.

We kept thinking we were doing the last series, but then Bob Larbey would write another one and Syd Lotterby always had such a lovely crew to work with. Even after we finally called it a day in 2002, we were suddenly asked back to make two Specials for Christmas 2005.

Jean in *As Time Goes By* with Geoffrey Palmer as Lionel, 1991–2002

The most hair-raising bit of all when filming a sitcom is when
you have to go out in front of an audience and say hello to
them; that's more taxing than doing the rest of the show.

As Time Goes By, 1991–2002

Geoffrey Palmer is fishing mad. In fact, it's often quite difficult to get him to work as he's always chasing the mayfly! So I bought him this special catch. It takes a lot of people behind the cameras to put even just a couple of us on the screen. On the next page you can see how many. The director Syd Lotterby (in the armchair front left) managed to get most of the same team together for each series, and a lot of them came back for two Christmas Specials in 2005. Syd has directed every single episode and they really all do it for him. So do we.

Ian Richardson and I had just taken part in a big fundraising gala for the Yvonne Arnaud Theatre in Guildford in 1996. The rehearsal seemed to go on for ever and didn't end until 6.30 p.m. So I went round all the dressing rooms, collecting guesses at fifty pence a go, on what time the actual gala performance would finish. Then we had a party onstage afterwards, and it looks here as if Ian might have won the jackpot.

The ABSA (now known as Arts & Business) Awards are usually held at the National Theatre, and often the Guest of Honour is a member of the Royal Family. As members of the National Theatre Company at the time, Edward Petheridge and I were presented to the Princess of Wales.

Our first holiday in Barbados was wonderfully relaxing. We read something like twenty-seven books in this amazingly short time. We just lay about, and read, and slept. I wasn't allowed to get a tan though, because of a part coming up, so here I am avoiding the sun.

I won the Tony (the Antoinette Perry Award) for *Amy's View* on Broadway in 1999. Finty came over and we all got ready in my dressing room at the Barrymore Theater.

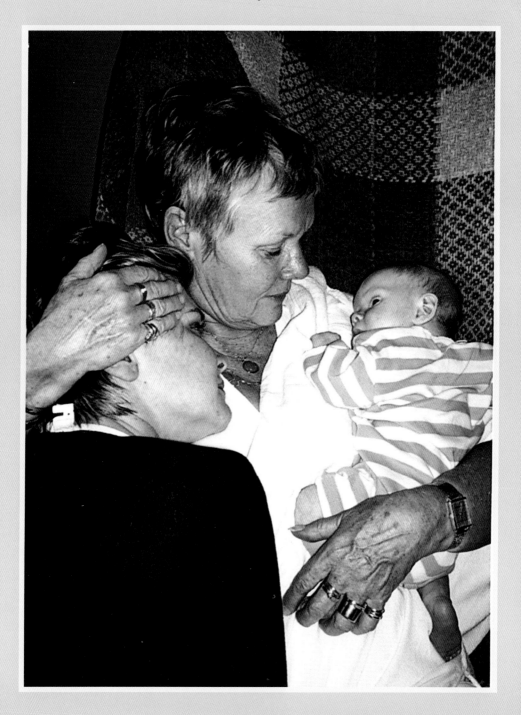

Finty and Sammy

OPPOSITE Three generations of Williamses when Sammy
was just two weeks old

We had a lovely christening party for Sammy, but it looks as if at least two of us needed a rest after it!

For Michael's birthday one year, I gave him this armillary sphere, which tells the time like a sundial. I had it made with all our initials and names on it, and Sammy was born just beforehand, so his name was added. Michael loved it. For my birthday, Finty had a ring of stone put round it inscribed with, 'When we are together, there is nothing we cannot achieve', which is something Michael used to say. When I came home for my birthday there were a lot of friends here and a trail of red wool all the way down through the meadow to the sphere; it was a beautiful surprise.

I loved playing Esmé in David Hare's play *Amy's View* at the National and then had a thrilling time on Broadway with it, but it didn't start out like that. For the very first time in my career I found I couldn't just pick up the lines in rehearsal and had to really work at it. I used to come home, say hello to Mike, go up and run a bath, and get into the bath with the script. I would spend an hour in the bath, just trying to learn a page. I don't like working like that, but it was a necessity. David attended nearly all the rehearsals and was a most encouraging audience for us, as he laughed at all the jokes.

Esmé in *Amy's View* with Samantha Bond as Amy,
Lyttelton Theatre and Aldwych, 1997

In rehearsal with Richard Eyre and David Hare

John Timbers took this picture of me making up for *Amy's View* the night before I flew off to my first Oscar ceremony.

'I feel for only eight minutes on the screen I should only get a little bit of him.'

I never expected to win the Oscar. Then, just before it was announced by Robin Williams, whom we'd met at Billy Connolly's, Michael squeezed my hand and said, 'Watch out, I think this is you.' I don't remember very much after that except Robin curtsying. I gave the Oscar to Michael to bring home and I went to the airport in Los Angeles, as I was flying to New York for *Amy's View*.

When he got back home he took Oscar to the pub!

Queen Elizabeth I in *Shakespeare in Love*, 1998

ABOVE As caricatured by Clive Francis

Franco Zeffirelli's film *Tea with Mussolini* was the first time I worked with Joan Plowright and we became great friends. The dog always looked at its trainer off-set whichever way we were looking in front of the camera. Finty and Sammy came out to Italy to join me, and we all took it in turns pushing the pram in the evening.

I love this picture. It was so nice to work with Franco Zeffirelli again, so many years after *Romeo and Juliet* at the Old Vic. Joan Plowright refused to stay in the hotel we were booked into in Rome, saying: 'My dear, it's a knocking-shop, I heard a couple of them at it as I went upstairs!' She took me off to the magnificent Hotel Eden, where Maggie Smith joined us; the production company weren't at all happy about paying the extra cost, but gave in when we went on strike about doing any press interviews until they did.

With Franco Zeffirelli and Joan Plowright at the premiere
of *Tea with Mussolini*, 1999

I had a line in Eduardo de Filippo's play *Filumena*, 'I don't suppose you know those hovels in San Giviniello, in Vergine, in Forcella, Tribunale, Palinetto...' and I totally dried on the First Night. Fortunately I had just come back from filming *Tea with Mussolini* in Italy, so I said instead, '...in Fusilli, Vermicelli, Valpolicella...' a lot of wine and food, mostly pasta, because I'd been having it for nearly three months. Not many people seemed to notice, but a couple of the critics recognised that something had gone wrong.

I was involved in *Men in Scarlet*, the son et lumière about the Chelsea Pensioners in 2000. At the press conference on the opening night one young man asked unwisely why we had all bothered to take part in such a show, and Ian Richardson barked back, 'Because these men are all heroes!' He was in sparkling form and kept us all amused as you can see.

Ian Richardson makes everyone laugh. Left to right: John Miller (producer), Ian Richardson, Martin Jarvis, Sir Jeremy Mackenzie (Governor of the Royal Hospital) and a helpless me

OPPOSITE *Filumena* with Michael Pennington as Domenico, Piccadilly, 1998

The developers of this site on the South Bank discovered the foundations of what proved to be the Rose Theatre, quite near the site of the Globe Theatre, also from the time of Shakespeare. The archaeologists found that the tiring-house faced the other way from what had previously been thought, and the hazelnuts in the floor were something to do with the drainage. When the builders proposed to bring the lorries in and demolish these foundations we all planned to lie down in front of them to stop them. We picked up Peggy Ashcroft very early that morning from her house in Hampstead, and brought her down to the Rose. They certainly weren't going to drive over her, and the site was preserved for viewing under the new building above it. She was a wonderfully forthright person, and a dear friend. Dustin Hoffman was also at this protest, and I reminded him of it when we were filming together in 2014.

Reopening the Shakespeare Birthplace Trust in 2000 was such a lovely day. Michael and I went back to Stratford so often after we had moved away, we spent so many happy years there; we were thrilled to be asked to cut the ribbon on this occasion, even if that proved a little more difficult in practice than we had anticipated.

TOP With Peggy Ashcroft and Michael at the site of the original Rose Theatre, 15 May 1989

BELOW With Michael at the Shakespeare Birthplace Trust, Stratford-Upon-Avon, 2000

With Richard Eyre at the Bafta Fellowship Awards, 2001

I was very worried about the BAFTA Fellowship Award evening in 2001 but Billy Connolly and Jim Broadbent made it easier by sending me up rotten. Jim said he hoped he had got my career back on track with *Iris* and described discovering what he called, 'the real Judi. Who of you knew, for instance, that she is over six foot tall and massively built? How many of you are aware that her strong Birmingham-Russian accent, which she so valiantly struggles to overcome in her stage and screen work, is in real life almost impenetrable? And it is a mark of her extreme professionalism that it was the very last week of filming before I even realised she had a prosthetic limb.' I'm glad there were a few jokers. Mind you, quite a lot of Billy's jokes had to be edited out before the show could be broadcast.

When I won the BAFTA Best Actress Award for *Mrs Brown* in 1998, it was stolen before I had even left the hotel at the end of the evening. BAFTA replaced it so quickly I wondered if this happened all the time. It just shows you can't be too careful.

With Billy Connolly and John Hurt at the BAFTA Fellowship Awards, 2001

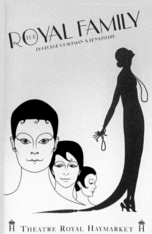

ROYAL FAMILY
BY GEORGE S. KAUFMAN & EDNA FERBER

H THEATRE ROYAL HAYMARKET **H**

Toby Stephens

Julia McKenzie

Philip Voss

Judi Dench, Toby Stephens, Philip Voss, Peter Bowles & Julia McKenzie

Robert Petkoff & Emily Blunt

Harriet Walter

Peter Bowles

Judi Dench

John Griffiths

Harriet Walter, Julia McKenzie, Emily Blunt & Judi Dench

Harriet Walter & Peter Blythe

Peter Hall

Penny Ryder

Joy Richardson

We enjoyed ourselves so much in *The Royal Family*. Here Toby Stephens and I are both being a bit over-dramatic. Toby played it very Douglas Fairbanks – a lot of swashbuckling on the stairs.

With Toby Stephens in *The Royal Family*, Theatre Royal, Haymarket, 2001

Celebrating Sammy's second birthday in New York at my apartment at the Sutton, when I was doing *Amy's View* on Broadway. I adore this picture.

I took this picture on the shore at Eriska overlooking Lismore and I love it. I think this visit started Sammy's feelings for Scotland too – he loves to go back there.

The costumes in *The Importance of Being Earnest* were incredible. I was wearing two foxes who looked as if they were having a fight over my shoulders. I couldn't get into any car to go up from the car park to the house, because my hat was so high, so they gave me a wonderful golf buggy. One of the locals must have seen me, because a friend of Geoffrey Palmer's, Ivor Herbert, sent me a copy of the parish magazine which recorded in its diary:

Spotted at West Wycombe:

5 Buzzards riding the wind over village (23 May)

Fox crossing West Wycombe Hill Road, A4010 side,
*   8.45 a.m. (24 May)*

Bar-Headed Geese, Lang Meadow (28 May)

Heard Cuckoo in flight, West Wycombe Hill, 8.30 a.m. (31 May)

Long-eared owl, A4010 side of West Wycombe Hill (3 June)

Dame Judi Dench in costume, main gate of Park (6 June)

Stoat chasing rabbit in the cricket meadow (8 June)

I loved the billing – after the long-eared owl, but before the stoat.

Lady Bracknell in *The Importance of Being Earnest*, 2001

Rupert Everett was adorable to play opposite in *The Importance of Being Earnest*, and great fun.

With Kevin Spacey and Peter O'Toole at the premiere for *The Shipping News*, 2001. Peter looks startled, I look somewhat taken aback by whatever someone is saying to us, only Kevin looks relaxed.

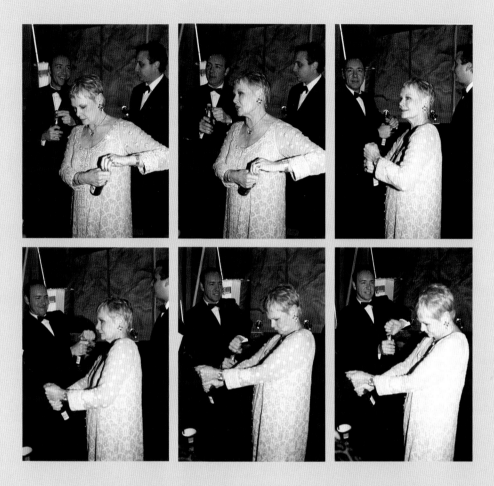

I've never had trouble with a bottle of champagne until the premiere of *The Shipping News*. Kevin Spacey was no help on this occasion!! I've never seen the film, but I loved making it with Kevin. That's where I saw icebergs for the first time. They are pure white, and inside they are bright turquoise. Flying over them is spellbinding.

Jim and I had a very similar sense of the absurd, and we laughed a lot between takes in *Iris*, which actually helped us to play some of those scenes.

I discovered that we shared a love of cats. His was called Naughty and I said, 'Oh, what a great name for a cat.'

'Not so hot when you're sitting in the vet's waiting-room with a whole lot of people, and they come out and call Naughty Broadbent!'

It was wonderful when he won the Oscar for best supporting actor, there was a lot of excitement in our corner.

Iris Murdoch in *Iris* with Jim Broadbent as John Bayley, 2001

We have always loved cats. Mitts, Spider, Newps, Fossil (in the barrow). Newps was short for Newspaper, also known as the great flat-footed Newps.

All the cats have been great explorers, especially Fossil. As soon as I put him down he was off into the wheelbarrow or whatever caught his interest. Fossil was particularly intrigued by the egg basket. Fortunately he never broke any of the eggs.

Sammy's first time as a pageboy (above right) was at the wedding of Sarah Kavanaugh to Kit Bingham. He was told he could have Tracy Island if he walked up the aisle and behaved very, very well. The children behaved impeccably and all went absolutely swimmingly until he said loudly, 'Now can I have *Thunderbirds*, Tracy Island?'

Opposite is my favourite picture of Sammy. For a very long time whenever you took a photo of him he mimed what you were doing.

Being at the Oxford Union in March 2002 was such good fun in the end, except it was frightening. I was so worried that I would be asked all sorts of highly intellectual questions that I said I would only do it if I could bring my biographer with me to take the chair. Then the first question from the floor was 'Who's your favourite James Bond?' and I thought this is going to be all right after all. Although in the photo below I look as though in a minute I'm going to ask John what I did, what was the play, what was the part and what was the date?

The Clintons came to see *The Breath of Life* one night. Madeleine Albright and Chelsea Clinton arrived at the beginning, but Bill Clinton and his wife only arrived at the interval. Somebody told me later that as President he became notorious for his unpunctuality.

Frances in *The Breath of Life* with Maggie Smith as Madeleine,
Theatre Royal, Haymarket, 2002

I didn't know *All's Well That Ends Well*, and I had never worked with Greg Doran before. The Countess is a wonderful part, and it's a wonderful play, and I just loved being back at Stratford as part of that Company. I have so many friends there, and I know the area so well, it was just lovely.

I hadn't been back to Stratford in a play for more than twenty years and it was Finty who talked me into it. She said she had such happy memories of growing up there that she wanted Sammy to have the same experience. We had one of the happiest Christmases there, certainly since Michael died in 2001, and we felt very near him at Charlecote, where he is buried.

OVERLEAF The Countess in *All's Well That Ends Well* with its director, Greg Doran, Stratford, 2003

Shall I drive off into the sunset? This is a very flash photo of me and my very flash car. I don't drive it. I just lean against it. It makes me feel about twenty-nine.

Eight years after the first photo of the three generations of
Williamses when Sammy was just two weeks old, this time
with Minnie, the new Shih-Tzu.

After our early years at the Old Vic, Maggie Smith and I only worked together at long intervals until recently, when we have done a play and two films in rapid succession. Charles Dance was so assured that you would never have known *Ladies in Lavender* was his first film as director. The young Polish violinist we rescued from the seashore in Cornwall was played by a very good German actor, Daniel Brühl, and this photograph was taken by his interpreter, Georgia Oetker.

I've never seen *The Chronicles of Riddick*, but I get so sent up about it. Originally I went to have the camera test for it the day before I started, when my wig was almost down to my feet, and I had bright blue lenses. The next day they said, 'No, you can't wear the lenses because Vin wears them', and they cut my hair like this as if I was going to the Oscars. So I didn't really feel like I was meant to be − some kind of alien person.

ABOVE *Ladies in Lavender* with Maggie Smith, 2004

BELOW *The Chronicles of Riddick* with Vin Diesel, 2004

Peter Hall was launching this new theatre at Kingston, with a design based on Shakespeare's Globe, and asked me if I would host a fundraising gala, with a cast of many of our friends. It was produced by John Miller and Joe Harmston, and as you can see we had a very starry cast, including David Oyelowo, Michael Pennington, Colin Salmon, Sam West, Samantha Bond, Martin Jarvis, and Charles Dance, who are all in this picture. I don't know where Tim Pigott-Smith had got to, he was probably plotting to get the black glove back to me, which I had thrown at his feet in rehearsal (see final picture and story at the end of the book).

I guess the title *One Knight Only* came from having just one knight in the cast, Antony Sher, with a supporting cast of dames: Joan Plowright, Helen Mirren, Eileen Atkins, Diana Rigg, and me.

ABOVE The Rose in Kingston Gala, 2004

OPPOSITE *One Knight Only*, Theatre Royal Haymarket, 2005

Hay Fever was heaven, every single performance; I adored it. It was rather like *Private Lives*: you think you're having a love affair every night. It was such good fun.

ABOVE Judith in *Hay Fever* with Belinda Lang, William Chubb, Peter Bowles, Dan Stevens and Kim Medcalf, Theatre Royal, Haymarket, 2006

OPPOSITE In rehearsal for *One Knight Only*. I have no recollection whatsoever of this gesture, or what I was doing, or what it means. Such over-acting!

Judith in *Hay Fever* with Peter Bowles as David, Theatre Royal, Haymarket, 2006

One night of *Hay Fever* Peter Bowles said: 'Jane Seymour drove out of the Champs-Élysées in her Hispano-Suiza.' We corpsed so badly that the audience caught on, we got into terrible trouble. Then of course he had to say the line again, we could see it coming. I can't remember what her name was meant to be, but it certainly wasn't Jane Seymour.

Tim Pigott-Smith came one night, and he sent the black glove to Dan Stevens, but I heard he was in, so I came in at the beginning with those gardening gloves on, one black and one green. In the interval Tim sent Dan a message, 'Well done! Very, very well done!!' Dan said, 'What do you mean? I haven't given it to her yet.'

Playing the saxophone in *Last of the Blonde Bombshells,* 2000

I've still got one of those. We had to rehearse a lot to get the fingering right; Kathy Stobart from Humphrey Lyttelton's Band taught me. I'd love to be able to play it properly, and now I regret that I didn't go on playing it. But whenever I just about got through a scale on it in my house, everybody left – the cats, the dog, Sammy, Michael, everybody.

We all had such fun with *The Merry Wives of Windsor*, though I'm not sure it was as much fun for the audience as it was for us. Perhaps they should make more musicals out of Shakespeare, though I'm not so sure about *Macbeth the Musical*!

Falstaff was originally supposed to be played by Desmond Barrit, but he had something wrong with his toe and had to drop out midway through rehearsals. So Simon Callow came in at very short notice. He was so good, because singing, which came easily to Des Barrit, didn't come so easily to Simon. We missed Des, but my goodness Simon was just terrific, and such good fun. My brother Jeff was Robert Shallow, and Brendan O'Hea played Pistol.

ABOVE Mistress Quickly in *The Merry Wives of Windsor* musical, with Alexandra Gilbreath as Mistress Ford and Haydn Gwynne as Mistress Page, Stratford, 2006

OPPOSITE Lovely get-up, isn't it?

OVERLEAF With Simon Callow as Falstaff

I had never worked with Bob Hoskins before, it was a complete joy. I had worked for Stephen Frears several times, and I so enjoyed making *Mrs Henderson Presents* that I never wanted it to end. I played the woman who bought the Windmill Theatre and employed Vivian van Damm, played by Bob.

Mrs Henderson Presents with Bob Hoskins, 2005

Barbara in *Notes on a Scandal* with Cate Blanchett as Sheba, 2006

I enjoyed doing *Notes on a Scandal*, it was a cracker to play, I loved it, and Richard Eyre was wonderful directing it.

When Cate Blanchett and I had the fight at the end of the film I had a back-brace put inside my costume, like a tortoise-shell, for when I was smashed against the book-case.

Cate had a bottle of champagne ready, and we opened it as soon as we finished the scene – we were very ready for that.

Cranford had such a large female cast, including Eileen Atkins, Francesca Annis, Lisa Dillon, Michelle Dockery, Emma Fielding, Celia Imrie, Lesley Manville and Finty, that the producer Sue Birtwistle christened us The Amazons. Much of the location work was shot at Lacock in Wiltshire, which still has the right period look.

The hedge had to be clipped first if three not-excessively-tall actresses were to be seen! It was nice to see a bit of sunshine that day, because it rained so much at Lacock during the shoot.

OPPOSITE *Cranford* with Julia McKenzie, 2007.

OVERLEAF Five Amazons at the window. Left to right: Julia McKenzie, Barbara Flynn, me, Deborah Findlay and Imelda Staunton

We had to have fake snow laid for this night scene; here we all are, acting cold. Lacock is such a beautiful place, but I don't think the people who live there ever have it to themselves.

I had worked with most of the cast before. They had set up an amazingly complicated scene, where the carriage came round the corner, and we had to come out of the cottage, when Eileen had to say 'Welcome to Cranford.' They had set it all up, sanded the road and everything. They said: 'Action, Eileen and Judi,' so we went out and Eileen said: 'Welcome to Ambridge.'

One of the nice perks of this show was having to go to Los Angeles to promote the screening of *Cranford* in America with Eileen Atkins and Imelda Staunton.

Dining scene with Michael Gambon, Lisa Dillon and Imelda Staunton

There was a lot of eating I remember, and we had to use these difficult period forks with only two prongs.

Lilli in *Nine*, 2009

Nine was good fun, except that I had to rehearse this song just as my great heroine Sophia Loren arrived on her first day, and she sat in the front row of this theatre set while I sang it, which I found rather frightening. Daniel Day-Lewis was playing the character based on Fellini, and the musical was based on his film *8½*. I hadn't worked with Dan since playing Gertrude to his Hamlet at the National in 1989, and it was good to work with him again.

ABOVE AND OVERLEAF *Madame de Sade* with Frances Barber and Deborah Findlay, Wyndham's Theatre, 2009

Rather a lot of frock in this production: we had to finish dressing at stage level, as we couldn't get down the stairs from the dressing rooms in them. It was done by three old Japanese actors shortly afterwards – quite right too. Frankie Barber had a line, 'My body was used as an altar.' Dead silence in the theatre, except for one voice, 'Oh, God!' from a dear friend of mine who was in that night.

My Week With Marilyn, 2011

Ken Branagh was playing Laurence Olivier and I was Sybil Thorndike in *My Week With Marilyn*. It was fun, but I was only in it for three days, because I was going off to work with Clint Eastwood. So the back of my head in the film is all Penny Ryder, doubling for me. I still haven't seen it. I have never been keen on watching myself onscreen, I always think I could have played the scene better, but now it's too late.

It looks as if I'm asking a question which Clint maybe doesn't want to answer. He didn't give me any notes at all, not once during *J. Edgar*. Once I was sitting on a bed, looking at some things, talking to Leo DiCaprio, then there was a pause, and I said, 'Are we about to go?' He said, 'We've been, we've shot it.' I loved the fact that he was such a quiet director, he doesn't like very much noise at all. There were no loud bells, or shouts of 'Quiet. Turn over. Action!' – it was all done with hand-signals, then Clint would just lean in and murmur, 'In your own time.' At the end instead of yelling, 'Cut!' he would just say quietly, 'Stop.'

With Clint Eastwood on the set of *J. Edgar*, 2011

It was lovely working with Clint, we never started before 9.30 in the morning, and we wrapped at 4 p.m. – you can't ask any more from a director. I once said to him, 'Do you think I could do this scene again?'

He said, 'Why?'

'We've just done two takes. I just feel maybe I could have another go at it.'

He said, 'OK, don't think.'

That's a wonderful note, because the more you do it, the more you stop to analyse it.

The costumes were very accurate, and very smart. My friend Pinkie Kavanaugh came out with me, and we stayed at the Four Seasons, it was like a holiday.

ABOVE Annie Hoover in *J. Edgar*, 2011   OPPOSITE With Leonardo DiCaprio

The Best Exotic Marigold Hotel is a lovely title for the film. The title suggested for the sequel was *The Second Best Exotic Marigold Hotel,* but I'm not sure if that will be agreed by the Americans, because of the possible interpretation.

The crowd scenes in India weren't difficult at all, they are all so used to film crews, and John Madden is such an extraordinary director and man.

Dev Patel had this lovely line: 'No more playing on the porch with the puppies, you are a big dog now.' He was a sweet boy.

The Best Exotic Marigold Hotel with Dev Patel, 2011

Look at all those wonderful colours!

In the back of a tuk tuk with Celia Imrie while filming the *The Best Exotic Marigold Hotel* in Jaipur.

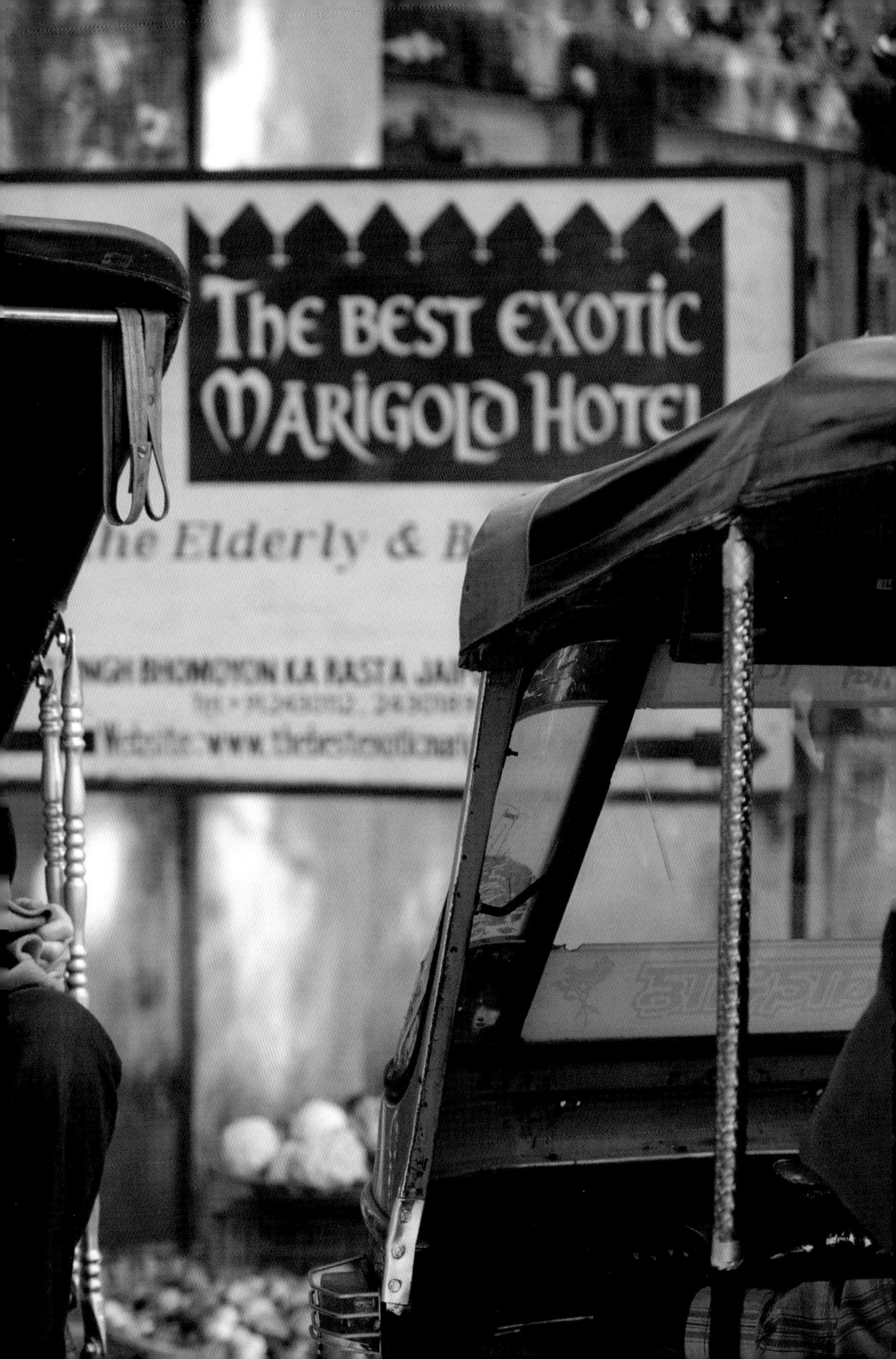
THE BEST EXOTIC
MARIGOLD HOTEL
Elderly &

Daniel Craig is hugely good fun. He does most of his stunts himself. He is very different from Pierce Brosnan, but both are really good actors, both with an enormous sense of humour, which I think is very important. If you take yourself too seriously in it, or in anything really, I think it's not good.

Casino Royale with Daniel Craig, my second James Bond, 2006

Skyfall with Daniel Craig, on location in Scotland, 2012

This was the only day we were actually in Glencoe filming *Skyfall*, though all the rest of those scenes looked as if they were. The mist stayed like that on the hills the whole day, it was very atmospheric.

It's not really a tattoo, it was made by Swarovski Crystal,
who gave me this transfer.

Skyfall premiere in the Royal Albert Hall, attended by the Prince of
Wales. That's when the front of my watch fell out.

Here Sam Mendes is giving me a couple of notes between takes for *Skyfall*. I had never forgotten his reaction when he first directed me in *The Cherry Orchard* in 1989. I said that I wasn't going to do something in one scene, I was going to try something else. He said, 'Well, you can if you want, but it won't work,' and he turned away and wouldn't watch. So at last I got my own back in *Skyfall*. When he said could he suggest something, I said, 'Well you can, but it won't work!'

During rehearsals for *Peter and Alice* I kept asking John Logan questions the whole time. Eventually, when he was sitting at the table and I kept leaning over to ask him questions about the script, he said: 'Now you see why I killed you off in *Skyfall.*' It was lovely working with Michael Grandage again.

With John Logan and Michael Grandage at the First Night Party
for *Peter and Alice*, 2013

Peter and Alice with Ben Whishaw, Noël Coward Theatre, 2013

I look staggeringly like my Auntie Cathy here. Ben played the young man on whom the character of Peter Pan was based, and I played the original model for Alice in *Alice in Wonderland*. The play opens with an actual meeting between the two real people, with lots of flashbacks and scenes from the books. Ben is such a good actor, I wish I'd seen him as Hamlet.

On an airport trolley filming *Philomena* with Steve Coogan, who co-wrote and co-produced the film and played Martin Sixsmith. Steve is the most brilliant mimic, and we had a lot of laughs during filming and afterwards. This scene was supposed to be taking place in Washington's Dulles Airport, but in fact we shot it at Stansted, and I got searched every time I came to film!

With Philomena Lee, whose story we filmed

Philomena Lee was in two minds about *Philomena* when she first saw it, but then said she approved of it. It was severely criticised by several Catholic organisations in America, who said it was an unpardonable attack on the Catholic Church. But then Harvey Weinstein arranged for Steve Coogan to accompany Philomena to Rome, where they were received by the Pope, which countered that disapproval. I would really have loved to have gone with them and met the Pope, but it was the day I came back from India for the BAFTA Awards, so I couldn't go.

OVERLEAF Those are the Mountains of Mourne sweeping down to the sea.

I had been invited on to Michael's show several times over the years, so was delighted to be asked on to his farewell programme with Billy Connolly. Neither of us knew what stories Billy would come up with, and he never disappointed us or the audience.

With Billy Connolly and Michael Parkinson, December 2007

My great friend David Mills accompanied me to the Venice Film Festival, and before the screening of *Philomena* he said to me, 'I think you're going to get a standing ovation.' I said, 'Don't be stupid, nobody gets a standing ovation for a film at Venice, nobody gets it.' He kept on, so I said, 'Oh David, it simply can't happen, I bet you.'

'OK, what's the bet?'

'The bet is, I'll bring you back to Venice and I'll pay for absolutely everything, you'll get a free holiday.'

'OK.'

It was a 12-minute standing ovation, I couldn't believe it!

'Will it be the six months?' he said.

With Stephen Frears at the Venice Film Festival, August 2013

Ken Branagh is a rare being. When he's directing he knows the first name of every single member of the crew. Here I am presenting him with the John Gielgud Golden Quill Award in 2000.

RIGHT Receiving an Honorary Degree from Leeds University in 2002. Melvyn Bragg is Chancellor of the University, and we both have very colourful robes. It's quite a get-up on these occasions.

BELOW Receiving an Honorary Degree from Oxford University in 2000. I'm wearing Mummy's brooch. The man behind me looks terribly glum!

ABOVE Receiving the Freedom of the City of London at the Guildhall in 2011. I'm sorry I haven't got my geese behind me, walking across the bridge, which is what the Freedom brings with it.

LEFT With Joan Plowright and David Hockney at A Celebration of the Arts at the Royal Academy of Arts in 2012. That was a good time. David told us, 'I don't really like this kind of do.'

At the National Theatre's Fiftieth Birthday Gala in 2013, we all did scenes from various earlier productions at the National. I sang 'Send in the Clowns' from *A Little Night Music,* and a short scene from *Antony and Cleopatra.* The whole evening was recorded for the BBC.

The rehearsals are worst for this kind of Gala, because you know that everyone else in the show is sitting out front watching you; it was ghastly to rehearse.

ABOVE LEFT Hampton Court Flower Show, 2010. They had created a new rose, and called it the Drama Queen Rose; I can't think why they presented it to me!

ABOVE RIGHT With David Mills at the Sandringham Flower Show, 2013. I don't know what the man behind us is up to.

With my brother Jeffery on the balcony of the Royal Shakespeare
Theatre in Stratford

My brother Jeff was one of the longest-serving members of the RSC, and when he died on 27 March 2014, Greg Doran that night called the whole Company – all the crew, wigs, wardrobe, actors, and he said, 'There's a great spirit gone.' He talked about Jeff and some of the parts he'd played, and when he said 'We ought to give him a big send-off,' they all broke into enormous applause and cheers. Then he wrote a letter to Jeff's wife Ann. It was the right thing to do, because Jeff had been a great member of the Company, and a great citizen of Stratford, he'd lived there since he was first married. I went down for the Memorial Service, and Greg gave a wonderful address.

With David, Finty and Sammy at the Shakespeare Globe Gala dinner, 2013

At the party after the BAFTA Awards, 2014. I was asked to fly back from India in the middle of filming, as I had been nominated for an Award for *Philomena,* but all in vain, as I didn't win. But it was a most enjoyable evening all the same.

I love the regular routine of the stage, and I'm always one of the first to arrive at the Stage Door. In the last few years I have been lucky enough to work again with old and dear friends, as well as making a number of new ones.

ABOVE Learning my lines in my dressing room at the Oxford Playhouse, 1965

OPPOSITE This looks as if I'm listening to a director, and probably disagreeing with him

I couldn't resist adding this picture to the others in this book. The saga of this little game with Tim Pigott-Smith has become quite well-known ever since John Miller wrote about it in his 1998 biography of me. At Peggy Ashcroft's Eightieth Birthday Gala in 1987, Tim was in a skit on *Jewel in the Crown* as Merrick, wearing one black glove. I made the mistake of joking to him, 'That's strangely attractive, that one-armed acting!' So the next night he wore one black glove when he came on as Octavius in *Antony and Cleopatra*. Later he slipped it into the basket with the asp, and it soon became a battle to see who could deliver it next to the other. I had this cake made for his birthday, and am currently cooking up another surprise for him. This running gag seems to amuse other people too, and whenever I do a Platform conversation with John someone in the audience always asks, 'Where is the black glove now?'

Chronology of Parts

THEATRE

Date	Play	Character	Theatre
1957	*York Mystery Plays*	Virgin Mary	St Mary's Abbey

The Old Vic Company, 1957–61

Date	Play	Character	Theatre
1957	*Hamlet*	Ophelia	Old Vic
	Measure for Measure	Juliet	Old Vic
	A Midsummer Night's Dream	First Fairy	Old Vic
1958	*Twelfth Night*	Maria	Old Vic and on tour to North America
	Henry V	Katherine	Old Vic and on tour to North America
1959	*The Double Dealer*	Cynthia	Old Vic
	As You Like It	Phebe	Old Vic
	The Importance of Being Earnest	Cecily	Old Vic
	The Merry Wives of Windsor	Anne Page	Old Vic
1960	*Richard II*	Queen	Old Vic
	Romeo and Juliet	Juliet	Old Vic and Venice Festival
	She Stoops to Conquer	Kate Hardcastle	Old Vic
	A Midsummer Night's Dream	Hermia	Old Vic

(And walk-ons in *King Lear* and *Henry VI*)

The Royal Shakespeare Company, 1961–2

Date	Play	Character	Theatre
1961	*The Cherry Orchard*	Anya	Aldwych
1962	*Measure for Measure*	Isabella	Stratford
	A Midsummer Night's Dream	Titania	Stratford
	A Penny for a Song	Dorcas Bellboys	Aldwych

The Nottingham Playhouse Company, 1963

Date	Play	Character	Theatre
1963	*Macbeth*	Lady Macbeth	Nottingham and tour to West Africa
	Twelfth Night	Viola	Nottingham and tour to West Africa
	A Shot in the Dark	Josefa Lautenay	Lyric

The Oxford Playhouse Company, 1964–5

Date	Play	Character	Theatre
1964	*Three Sisters*	Irina	Oxford
	The Twelfth Hour	Anna	Oxford
1965	*The Alchemist*	Dol Common	Oxford
	Romeo and Jeannette	Jeannette	Oxford
	The Firescreen	Jacqueline	Oxford

The Nottingham Playhouse Company, 1965–6

Date	Play	Character	Theatre
1965	*Measure for Measure*	Isabella	Nottingham
	Private Lives	Amanda	Nottingham
1966	*The Country Wife*	Margery Pinchwife	Nottingham
	The Astrakhan Coat	Barbara	Nottingham
	St Joan	Joan	Nottingham

The Oxford Playhouse Company, 1966–7

Date	Play	Character	Theatre
1966	*The Promise*	Lika	Oxford
	The Rules of the Game	Silia	Oxford
1967	*The Promise*	Lika	Fortune
1968	*Cabaret*	Sally Bowles	Palace

The Royal Shakespeare Company, 1969–71

Date	Play	Character	Theatre
1969	*The Winter's Tale*	Hermione/Perdita	Stratford
	Women Beware Women	Bianca	Stratford
	Twelfth Night	Viola	Stratford
1970	*London Assurance*	Grace Harkaway	Aldwych
	Major Barbara	Barbara Undershaft	Aldwych
1971	*The Merchant of Venice*	Portia	Stratford
	The Duchess of Malfi	Duchess	Stratford
	Toad of Toad Hall	Fieldmouse, Stoat and Mother Rabbit	Stratford
1973	*Content to Whisper*	Aurelia	Royal, York
	The Wolf	Vilma	Apollo, Queen's Playhouse, Oxford New London
1974	*The Good Companions*	Miss Trant	Her Majesty's
1975	*The Gay Lord Quex*	Sophy Fullgarney	Albery

The Royal Shakespeare Company, 1975–80

Date	Play	Character	Theatre
1975	*Too True to be Good*	Sweetie Simpkins	Aldwych
1976	*Much Ado About Nothing*	Beatrice	Stratford
	Macbeth	Lady Macbeth	Stratford, Donmar and Young Vic
	The Comedy of Errors	Adriana	Stratford
	King Lear	Regan	Stratford

1977	*Pillars of the Community*	Lona Hessel	Aldwych
1978	*The Way of the World*	Millamant	Aldwych
1979	*Cymbeline*	Imogen	Stratford
1980	*Juno and the Paycock*	Juno Boyle	Aldwych
1981	*A Village Wooing*	Young Woman	New End

The National Theatre Company, 1982

Date	Play	Character	Theatre
1982	*The Importance of Being Earnest*	Lady Bracknell	Lyttelton
	A Kind of Alaska	Deborah	Cottesloe
1983	*Pack of Lies*	Barbara Jackson	Lyric

The Royal Shakespeare Company, 1984–5

Date	Play	Character	Theatre
1984	*Mother Courage*	Mother Courage	Barbican
1985	*Waste*	Amy O'Connell	Barbican and Lyric
1986	*Mr and Mrs Nobody*	Carrie Pooter	Garrick

The National Theatre Company, 1987–91

Date	Play	Character	Theatre
1987	*Anthony and Cleopatra*	Cleopatra	Olivier
	Entertaining Strangers	Sarah Eldridge	Cottesloe
1989	*Hamlet*	Gertrude	Olivier
	The Cherry Orchard	Ranevskaya	Aldwych
1991	*The Plough and the Stars*	Bessie Burgess	Young Vic
	The Sea	Mrs Rafi	Lyttelton
1992	*Coriolanus*	Volumnia	Chichester

The Royal Shakespeare Company, 1992

Date	Play	Character	Theatre
1992	*The Gift of the Gorgon*	Helen Damson	Barbican and Wyndham's

The National Theatre Company, 1994–8

Date	Play	Character	Theatre
1994	*The Seagull*	Arkadina	Olivier
1995	*Absolute Hell*	Christine Foskett	Lyttelton
	A Little Night Music	Desirée Armfeldt	Olivier
1997	*Amy's View*	Esmé	Lyttelton
1998	*Amy's View*	Esmé	Aldwych
1998	*Filumena*	Filumena	Piccadilly
1999	*Amy's View*	Esmé	Barrymore, New York
2001	*The Royal Family*	Fanny Cavendish	Theatre Royal, Haymarket
2002	*The Breath of Life*	Frances	Theatre Royal, Haymarket

The Royal Shakespeare Company, 2003

Date	Play	Character	Theatre
2003	*All's Well That End's Well*	The Countess	Swan, Stratford and Gielgud
2006	*Hay Fever*	Judith Bliss	Theatre Royal, Haymarket

The Royal Shakespeare Company, 2006

Date	Play	Character	Theatre
2006	*The Merry Wives of Windsor*	Mistress Quickly	Stratford
2009	*Madame de Sade*	The Marquise	Wyndham's
2010	*A Midsummer Night's Dream*	Titania	Rose, Kingston
2013	*Peter and Alice*	Alice	Noël Coward

DIRECTOR

Date	Title	Company/Venue
1988	*Much Ado About Nothing*	Renaissance Theatre Company
1989	*Look Back in Anger*	Renaissance Theatre Company
	Macbeth	Central School of Speech and Drama
1991	*The Boys from Syracuse*	Regent's Park Open Air Theatre
1993	*Romeo and Juliet*	Regent's Park Open Air Theatre

TELEVISION

Date	Title	Company
1959	*Family on Trial*	Associated Rediffusion
1960	*Z-Cars*	BBC
	Henry V – Age of Kings	BBC
1962	*Major Barbara*	BBC
1963	*The Funambulists*	ATV
1965	*Safety Man – Mogul*	BBC
1966	*Talking to a Stranger*	BBC
1968	*On Approval*	Yorkshire
1970	*Confession – Neighbours*	Granada
1972	*Luther*	BBC
1973	*Keep an Eye on Amelie*	BBC
1977	*The Comedy of Errors* (RSC)	Thames
1978	*Macbeth* (RSC)	Thames
	Langrishe Go Down	BBC
	A Village Wooing	Yorkshire
1979	*On Giant's Shoulders*	BBC
	Love in a Cold Climate	Thames
1980–3	*A Fine Romance*	London Weekend
1980	*The Cherry Orchard*	BBC
	Going Gently	BBC

1982	*Saigon: Year of the Cat*	Thames
1985	*The Browning Version*	BBC
	Mr and Mrs Edgehill	BBC
	Ghosts	BBC
1986	*Make and Break*	BBC
1988	*Behaving Badly*	Channel Four
1990	*Can You Hear Me Thinking?*	BBC
	The Torch	BBC
1991	*Absolute Hell*	BBC
1991–2002	*As Time Goes By*	BBC
1999	*The Last of the Blonde Bombshells*	BBC
2007–9	*Cranford*	BBC

FILMS

Date	Title	Director
1964	*The Third Secret*	Charles Crichton
1965	*He Who Rides a Tiger*	Charles Crichton
	A Study in Terror	James Hill
	Four in the Morning	Anthony Simmons
	A Midsummer Night's Dream	Peter Hall
1973	*Dead Cert*	Tony Richardson
1984	*Wetherby*	David Hare
1985	*A Room with a View*	James Ivory
1986	*84 Charing Cross Road*	David Jones
1987	*A Handful of Dust*	Charles Sturridge
1988	*Henry V*	Kenneth Branagh
1994	*Jack and Sarah*	Tim Sullivan
1995	*Goldeneye*	Martin Campbell
	Hamlet	Kenneth Branagh
1996	*Mrs Brown*	John Madden
1997	*Tomorrow Never Dies*	Roger Spottiswoode

1998	*Shakespeare in Love*	John Madden
1999	*Tea with Mussolini*	Franco Zeffirelli
	The World is Not Enough	Michael Apted
2000	*Chocolat*	Lasse Hallström
2001	*The Shipping News*	Lasse Hallström
	Iris	Richard Eyre
	The Importance of Being Earnest	Oliver Parker
2002	*Die Another Day*	Lee Tamahori
2004	*Ladies in Lavender*	Charles Dance
	The Chronicles of Riddick	Vin Diesel
2005	*Pride and Prejudice*	Joe Wright
	Mrs Henderson Presents	Stephen Frears
2006	*Casino Royale*	Martin Campbell
	Notes on a Scandal	Richard Eyre
2008	*Quantum of Solace*	Marc Forster
2009	*Nine*	Rob Marshall
	Rage	Sally Potter
2011	*Jane Eyre*	Cary Fukunaga
	My Week with Marilyn	Simon Curtis
	J. Edgar	Clint Eastwood
	The Best Exotic Marigold Hotel	John Madden
2012	*Skyfall*	Sam Mendes
2013	*Philomena*	Stephen Frears

Awards

Date   Award

1961 Paladino D'Argentino at the Venice Festival for *Romeo and Juliet*

1965 BAFTA Award, Most Promising Newcomer in Film for *Four in the Morning*

1968 BAFTA Award, Best Television Actress for *Talking to a Stranger*

1970 Ofcer of the Most Excellent Order of the British Empire

1977 Olivier (SWET) Award, Best Actress for *Macbeth*

1978 Honorary Doctor of Letters, Warwick University

1980 Olivier (SWET) Award, Best Actress for *Juno and the Paycock*

1980 Evening Standard Award, Best Actress for *Juno and the Paycock*

1980 Plays and Players Award, Best Actress for *Juno and the Paycock*

1980 Variety Club Actress of the Year Award

1982 BAFTA Award, Best Actress in Television for *A Fine Romance, Going Gently* and *The Cherry Orchard*

1982 Broadcasting Press Guild TV & Radio Award, Best Actress for *A Fine Romance*

1983 Honorary Doctor of Letters, University of York

1983 Evening Standard Award, Best Actress for *A Kind of Alaska*

1983 Plays and Players Award, Best Actress for *The Importance of Being Earnest*

1983 Olivier (SWET) Award, Best Actress for *Pack of Lies*

1984 Plays and Players Award, Best Actress for *Pack of Lies*

1985 BAFTA Award, Best Entertainment Performance Television for *A Fine Romance*

1986 BAFTA Award, Best Actress in a Supporting Role in Film for *A Room with a View*

1987 Olivier Award, Best Actress for *Antony and Cleopatra*

1987 Drama Magazine Award, Best Actress for *Antony and Cleopatra*

1987 Evening Standard Award, Best Actress for *Antony and Cleopatra*

1988 Dame Commander of the Most Excellent Order of the British Empire

1988 CableACE Award, Actress in a Theatrical or Dramatic Special for *The Browning Version*

1988 BAFTA Award, Best Actress in a Supporting Role in Film for *A Handful of Dust*

1996 Olivier Award, Best Actress for
Absolute Hell

1996 Olivier Award, Best Actress in a Musical
for *A Little Night Music*

1997 Evening Standard Awards Patricia
Rothermere Award for Distinguished Services
to Theatre

1997 Scottish BAFTA Award, Best Actress
for *Mrs Brown*

1997 BAFTA Award, Best Actress in Film
for *Mrs Brown*

1998 Golden Globe Award, Best Actress
in a Motion Picture for *Mrs Brown*

1998 Satellite Award, Best Actress for
Mrs Brown

1998 Critics Circle Award, Best Actress
for *Amy's View*

1998 National Society of Film Critics Award,
Best Supporting Actress for *Shakespeare in
Love*

1998 BAFTA Award, Best Actress in a
Supporting Role in Film for *Shakespeare
in Love*

1999 Screen Actors Guild Award,
Outstanding Performance by a Cast in a
Motion Picture for *Shakespeare in Love*

1999 Academy Award, Best Actress in a
Supporting Role for *Shakespeare in Love*

1999 Tony Award, Best Actress for
Amy's View

2000 Golden Globe Award, Best Actress
in a TV Movie for *The Last of the Blonde
Bombshells*

2000 Screen Actors Guild Award, Best
Supporting Actress for *Chocolat*

2001 BAFTA Award, Best Actress in
Television for *The Last of the Blonde Bombshells*

2001 BAFTA Academy Fellowship

2001 BAFTA Award, Best Actress in Film
for *Iris*

2004 Olivier Awards Society Special Award

2005 Companion of Honour

2007 WhatsOnStage Award, Best Actress
for *Hay Fever*

2007 British Independent Film Award,
Best Actress for *Notes on a Scandal*

2008 Satellite Award, Best Actress in a
Miniseries or Television Film for *Cranford*

2008 European Film Awards Lifetime
Achievement Award

2009 Satellite Awards Special Achievement
Award, Best Ensemble in a Motion Picture
for *Nine*

2011 Karlovy Vary International Film Festival
Crystal Globe Award for Outstanding
Artistic Contribution to World Cinema

2011 BFI Fellowship Award for Outstanding
Contribution to Film and Television

2011 Praemium Imperiale Laureate Award for
Film and Theatre

2012 Women Film Critics Circle Award,
Women's Work/Best Ensemble for *The Best
Exotic Marigold Hotel*

2013 Women Film Critics Circle Award,
Best Actress for *Philomena*

2014 Irish Film and Television Award,
Best International Actress for *Philomena*

2014 London Critics Circle Film Award,
British Actress of the Year for *Philomena*

Picture credits

Every effort has been made to trace or contact all copyright holders. The publishers would be pleased to rectify any errors or omissions brought to their attention at the earliest opportunity.

P i Yevonde Portrait Archive; ii Cecil Beaton / National Portrait Gallery; iv Linda Rosier / NY Daily News Archive via Getty Images; viii Mike McKeown / Daily Express / Hulton Archive / Getty Images; xiii Snowdon / Camera Press; xiv Yevonde Portrait Archive; 3-5 Judi Dench; 7 Tenniel Evans; 8-10 Judi Dench; 11 Tony Wallace Daily Mail / Rex; 13 John Timbers; 14 Wendy Toye; 15 Alex McCowen; 16 (top) Judi Dench (bottom) Chrispian Woodgate; 17-18 Judi Dench; 20 Joe Cocks Studio Collection / Shakespeare Birthplace Trust; 21 BBC; 22 Daily Express / Mander & Michenson Theatre Collection; 23 Tomas Jaski Ltd Mander & Michenson Theatre Collection; 24 Judi Dench; 25 BAFTA; 26-27 Judi Dench; 28 Ian Richardson / Joe Cocks Studio Collection; 29 (top) Filmways / Royal Shakespeare / The Kobal Collection (bottom) David Farrell Hulton Archive / Getty Images; 30 Nobby Clark / ArenaPAL / Topfoto; 31 ArenaPAL / Topfoto; 32 -33 Judi Dench; 34-35 Reg Lancaster Express / Getty Images; 36-37 Judi Dench; 38 Bentley Archive Popperfoto / Getty Images; 39 ArenaPAL / Topfoto; 41 Phillip Jackson / Associated Newspapers / Rex; 42-43 David Magnus / Rex; 44 (top) Ian Richardson / Joe Cocks Studio Collection (bottom) Joe Cocks Studio Collection / Shakespeare Birthplace Trust; 46-47 Morris Newcombe; 49-51 Tina Carr; 52 (left) Judi Dench (right) John Brook / Shakespeare Birthplace Trust; 53 John Timbers; 54 Judi Dench; 55 John Brook / Shakespeare Birthplace Trust; 56 Press Association; 57-61 Judi Dench; 63 (top) Zoe Dominic (middle and bottom) Nobby Clark; 65 Rex; 66 Solihull News; 67 Donald Cooper / Photostage; 69 (top) Joe Cocks Studio Collection / Shakespeare Birthplace Trust (bottom) ITV / Rex; 70 Joe Cocks Studio Collection / Shakespeare Birthplace Trust; 71 Sally Soames / The Sunday Times; 72 Donald Cooper / Photostage; 73-75 Judi Dench; 76 -77 Zoe Dominic; 78 David Hare; 79 Judi Dench; 80-81 John Timbers; 82 Judi Dench; 83 Yorkshire Post; 84 (top) London Weekend Television / Rex (bottom) Judi Dench; 85 Donald Cooper / Photostage; 86 Nobby Clark; 87 Donald Cooper / Photostage; 88-89 Reg Wilson / Royal Shakespeare Company; 90 BBC; 92-93 John Timbers; 94-95 Judi Dench; 96 Radio Times; 97 Granada Television; 98 Donald Cooper / Photostage; 100 John Haynes; 102 Douglas H. Jeffrey; 103 Nobby Clark; 104-107 Judi Dench; 108-9 John Haynes; 110-11 © Donald Cooper/Photostage 112 Mark Douet; 113 Moira Williams; 114-115 Donald Cooper / Photostage; 117 John Haynes; 118 David Gamble / Topfoto; 119 (top) John Timbers (bottom) The Royal National Theatre UK, Radio Times;121 John Haynes; 122 Henrietta Butler / ArenaPAL; 123 Judi Dench; 124 The Royal National Theatre UK; 125 Judi Dench; 126 Popperfoto/Getty Images; 128-130 Mark Tillie / Ecosse / Miramax; 131 Judi Dench; 132 Rex / Richard Young; 133 Keith Hamshire / Danjaq / Eon

/ UA / The Kobal Collection; 135-136 DLT Entertainment UK Limited; 137 John Timbers; 138-139 DLT Entertainment UK Limited; 140 (top) Ian Richardson (bottom) Bill Mackenzie / National Theatre Archive; 142-147 Judi Dench; 148 The Royal National Theatre UK; 149 John Haynes; 150-151 John Timbers; 152 (top) Clive Francis (bottom) Judi Dench; 153 R.Hepler / Everett / Rex; 154 Judi Dench; 155 (top) Everett Collection / Rex (bottom) AKG Images; 157 Rex; 158 Alistair Muir; 159 John Miller; 161 (top) Topfoto (bottom) Newsteam Syndication; 162-163 BAFTA; 164 The Peter Hall Company and the Theatre Royal Haymarket; 165 Donald Cooper / Photostage; 166-167 Judi Dench; 168-169 Greg Williams / Art & Commerce; 170 (top) Rex (bottom) Press Association; 171 BAFTA; 172 Rex; 174-177 Judi Dench; 178 Eddie Gallacher and the Oxford Union; 179 (left) Stewart Mark / Camera Press (right) Dave Benett / Getty Images; 180 RSC Martin Norris; 182-183 Donald Cooper / Photostage; 184 Judi Dench;185 John Timbers; 187 (top) Georgia Oetker (bottom) Universal / The Kobal Collection / Lederer; 188 Alan Weller Film Magic / Getty Images; 189-190 Judy Totton / Rex; 191 Nigel Norrington / Camera Press; 192 Ferdaus Shamim WireImage / Getty Images; 193 Everett Collection / Rex; 194 Nigel Norrington ArenaPAL / Topfoto; 195 Alastair Muir / Rex; 196-197 Nigel Norrington ArenaPAL / Topfoto; 198-199 Stephen Frears; 200 20th Century Fox / Everett / Rex; 201 Giles Keyte / Fox Searchlight / The Kobal Collection; 202 BBC; 203 Matt Cardy / Getty Images; 204-205 BBC; 206 Matt Cardy / Getty Images; 207 (top) Yoram Kahana Shooting Star / Camera Press (bottom) BBC; 208 Lucamar Productions / The Kobal Collection; 209 Marilyn Kingwill ArenaPAL / Topfoto; 210-211 Johan Persson ArenaPAL / Topfoto; 212 Weinstein / Everett / Rex; 213 Malpaso / Warner Bros / The Kobal Collection; 214 Warner Bros / Everett Collection / Rex; 215 Rex; 216 Foxsearch / Everett / Rex; 217 Blueprint Pictures / The Kobal Collection; 218-219 Photos 12 / Alamy; 220-221 Jay Maidment / Eton / Danjaq / Sony / The Kobal Collection; 222 Col Pics / Everett / Rex; 223 (top) Dave Hogan / Getty Images (bottom) Rex; 224 Danjaq / Eon Production / The Kobal Collection; 226 Dan Woollen / Rex; 227 Johan Persson ArenaPAL /Topfoto; 228 Snap Stills / Rex; 229 Doug Peters/EMPICS Entertainment Press Association; 230-231 Moviestore / Rex; 232 Ken McKay / Rex; 233 Domenico Stinellis / AP / Press Association; 234 William Conran / PA Archive / Press Association Images; 235 (top) Theodore Wood / Camera Press (middle left) Dave Hartley /Rex (middle right) Tony Kyriacou / Rex (bottom) Jane Mingay / Rex; 236 Catherine Ashmore; 237 (left) Paul Grover / Rex (right) Rex; 238 Mark Williamson; 240 David Benett / Getty Images; 241 Ian West / PA Wire / Press Association; 242 Mark Douet / ArenaPAL; 243 Associated Newspapers / Rex; 245 Judi Dench

First published in Great Britain in 2014 by Weidenfeld & Nicolson
an imprint of the
Orion Publishing Group Ltd
First U.S. Edition: November 2014

1 3 5 7 9 10 8 6 4 2

A CIP catalogue record for this book is available
from the British Library.

ISBN: 978-1-250-07111-8 (hardcover)
ISBN: 978-1-4668-8219-5 (e-book)

Designed by carrdesignstudio.com
Printed and bound in Italy

www.stmartins.com

MIX
Paper from
responsible sources
FSC® C015829
FSC
www.fsc.org